"Lloyd manages to demystify the entrepreneurial process by showing the reader how others have turned the "impossible dream" into an attainable goal. His practical nuts-and-bolts approach should inspire many who are considering taking the entrepreneurial "leap." Should be on the standard reading list for business schools and entrepreneurial classes."

—PHILLIP MATTHEWS
Owner and President
Bell Sports and
Chairman
Wolverine

"Entrepreneurs no longer have to dream the impossible dream. *Entrepreneurs Are Made Not Born* documents the experience, explores the character traits, and unravels the mysteries of entrepreneurship. Chapter by chapter it becomes clear how the possibilities of dreams can be turned into the possibilities of action. I recommend this book to anyone looking for insights or understanding of the entrepreneurial process."

—RON RASHKOW
Founder
Handy Andy Home
Improvement Center

"I wish I had read this book years before I founded UDC. So many things that took me years to learn are in *Entrepreneurs Are Made Not Born*. That Lloyd Shefsky captured the spirit and joy of doing your own thing attests to his totally unique perspective and knowledge."

—GARY ROSENBERG
Founder
UDC Homes

"Lloyd has captured the essence of the entrepreneurial spirit. His focus on entrepreneurs highlights their significant role in our economy, plus providing role models for the future."

—DAVE DIETERLE
Executive Director
Illinois Council on Economic
Education

"Shefsky understands that successful entrepreneurs are just ordinary people with extraordinary determination."

—MARY KAY ASH
Founder
Mary Kay Cosmetics

"Lloyd is a great entrepreneur himself. His book is a must read for others who wish to follow in the footsteps of Lloyd's highly successful clients."

—NEILL BROWNSTEIN
General Partner
Bessemer Venture Partners

"To me, founders are the most important people—whether founding a hospital, a country, a business. They put in motion the opportunities for others. Stimulating entrepreneurs as the book does is a noble purpose."

—ROBERT W. GALVIN
Chairman
Motorola, Inc.

"Lloyd Shefsky's new book truly captures the entrepreneurial spirit. *Entrepreneurs Are Made Not Born* will inspire up-and-coming business leaders to success through vision, creativity and hard work."

—WILLIAM F. FARLEY
Founder
Farley Industries

Entrepreneurs Are Made Not Born

Lloyd E. Shefsky

McGraw-Hill, Inc.

New York   San Francisco   Washington, D.C.   Auckland   Bogotá
Caracas   Lisbon   London   Madrid   Mexico City   Milan
Montreal   New Delhi   San Juan   Singapore
Sydney   Tokyo   Toronto

Library of Congress Cataloging-in-Publication Data

Shefsky, Lloyd E.
    Entrepreneurs are made not born / Lloyd E. Shefsky.
        p.   cm.
    Includes index.
    ISBN 0-07-057025-6
    1. Entrepreneurship.   2. New business enterprises.   3. Success in
business.   I. Title.
HB615.S495   1994
658.4'21—dc20   93-46213
                                                    CIP

  2 3 4 5 6 7 8 9 0 DOC/DOC 9 0 9 8 7 6 5 4

ISBN 0-07-057025-6

*The sponsoring editor for this book was Caroline Carney, the editing supervisor
was Jane Palmieri, and the production supervisor was Donald Schmidt. It was
set in Palatino by McGraw-Hill's Professional Book Group composition unit.*

Printed and bound by R. R. Donnelley & Sons Company.

This book is printed on recycled, acid-free paper containing a minimum of 50% recycled de-inked fiber.

To Dawn, Julie, and Doug
Be good, make things happen

To Natalie
Who makes good things happen

To Mom and Dad
*Who did good making me happen to be an
entrepreneur*

Contents

Preface

Are you aware that some people jump out of bed to rush to their jobs every day, almost always work past "quitting time," and often skip meals, social plans, and sleep in order to spend more time at work? Why do these people behave in such an unusual way? Because they have the toughest of bosses and they love their jobs. They may be labeled "workaholics" by their less motivated associates, but they are not. They are, in fact, entrepreneurs. As their own bosses, they are self-administering task masters, whose common goal is the fervent pursuit of their own beloved dreams.

Are you that enthusiastic about your job? Here's a simple test to help you find out. Ask yourself, "What's the opposite of work?" If you say "fun," "happiness," or "enjoyment," you have a problem—you are spending 35 or more hours a week in an unhappy endeavor.

Why would you willingly commit yourself and nearly 100,000 hours of your life to something that you don't enjoy? Perhaps you think you have no choice. After all, you must work for a living, an ominous and gloomy mandate. The issue is not working hard, it is liking what you do. Even if you like the kind of work you do, you may not enjoy it because you work for someone else instead of for yourself.

Many employees work from 9 to 5 because their bosses tell them they must. Does this sound like you? If you were an entrepreneur, you could decide to work from 5 to 9 instead. And whether 5 to 9 is four hours or sixteen hours would be totally up to you. Because you could choose to do what it takes to achieve your dream, rather than what it takes to satisfy some bureaucrat's rule or your boss's dictates.

Ah, but there are risks, you say. You have reasons—the mortgage, the kids, your seniority, your pension—that make you cling to the security of your job. How could you threaten that security? Sounds reasonable, but thousands who were fired, laid off, or caught in a restructuring clung to that same "security." And although entrepreneurs do take risks, they also are free to decide which risks to take and how to deal with them. The reasons that make you cling to your job aren't reasons at all but excuses and emotional barriers. You can learn to overcome them.

Think about learning to ride a bike. This alternative to walking seems unsteady and perilous. Once you start riding, however, balance is easy, the "work" of pedaling is fun, and you become a free spirit because the brakes, gears, and pedals are all under your control. Once you know how to ride, how do you describe the thrill of the speed or rush of wind in your face or the pride of achievement? Well, it's often just as difficult for an entrepreneur to explain the thrill of entrepreneurship. I've talked with hundreds of them, and I can show you how they think and how you can love your work as much as they do.

I can teach you to become entrepreneurial. You have what it takes. You just need to learn how to capitalize on your own latent talent and traits. Learning how to become an entrepreneur may not be as simple as learning to ride a bike, but it is easier than you think. It will enrich your life immeasurably. Before you know it, you'll start describing your work as fun.

In Horace Greeley's day, a young man could easily find a life of romance, excitement, and success by going West. Life is more complicated today. The Old West is gone, and the new frontiers—space, oceans, technology—are usually too complex for an individual to conquer alone. But the American Dream still exists, stronger than ever, and its requirements are less restrictive. You don't have to be young or a man. Anyone can be an entrepreneur.

I had a good boss but decided to pick a better one—myself. I did it nearly 25 years ago, yet the memory is as clear as this morning's sunrise. There were three of us that first day at our new firm: my partner, our associate, and myself. When my partner walked in the office, he exclaimed, "It's only 6:30 a.m. and I'm the third one in the office!" We were all so excited and eager to get started in our new venture. Our adrenaline was flowing; the world was full of promise and excitement.

Leaving my job wasn't easy. My boss was my manager and mentor. We had a solid relationship, built on mutual respect. Although I was only 29, my boss had assured me that, some day, the firm would belong to me. He even made me his partner. Aside from the security of my job, I had to consider my financial situation. Young lawyers didn't earn much then, and I had many more years of payments due on my tuition loans, a mortgage, and a new baby to support. My clients were few and, for the most part, start-ups with insufficient capital. I really couldn't afford to hire myself. Besides, I had so much going for me where I was. But I wanted to be my own boss, and so I had to leave.

When I struck out on my own, people congratulated me, which made me proud, even though I wondered, at first, why. They wouldn't be there when I signed notes at the bank or when I held my paycheck until enough fees came in to cover it. They'd still be in bed at 5:30 a.m., as I arrived at my office, and they'd be home or out with friends, evenings and weekends, while I was busy being both boss and employee. And, most of all, the jury was out on whether I would succeed or fail. But, now, I understand their praise. Some enjoyed my adventure because they had become their own bosses and were reliving the experience vicariously. Others regretted that they could not do what I was doing; they could only dream of becoming their bosses.

Some people take up hobbies, such as Outward Bound survival games, parachuting, or bungee jumping, to develop and test their skills of bravery, discipline, endurance, perseverance, confidence, creativity, competitiveness, commitment, and focus. I wanted to combine all those traits and sought a shortcut by becoming an entrepreneur.

I wasn't oblivious to the risks, but risks paled next to the opportunities—not just to earn more but to be tested, every day, as an individual and to know that my success depended on and would flow from my own talents and efforts. And, most of all, to know I did it myself and would benefit accordingly. The burdens were very real, but they reminded me of an old ad for Boys Town—the picture of the boy carrying a younger boy on his back and saying, "He ain't heavy; he's my brother." When I became my own boss, my new business didn't seem heavy, because it was my baby. Very little in my life has been more exciting than selecting myself as my new boss.

Think about your own situation. Do you love what you do and how you do it? Or do you hate getting up for work every day? Is it your boss or your job? Do you feel you could do the job better than your boss does? Thirty-seven percent of Americans feel they could. Do you hate, as one of my clients put it, to mortgage your future to someone else's stupidity when you have plenty of your own? Does it bother you that your boss controls your destiny? Are you frustrated by giving your all to your employer while knowing you could be laid off if things get tight or someone else seems to be better at your job than you? What happens to your job if someone makes the company's owners an offer they can't refuse? Maybe you have the wrong boss.

I have interviewed 200 entrepreneurs for this book and represented hundreds more as a lawyer during the last 25 years. What I have learned from them can help you. Their stories of success and failure in almost every industry and business throughout the country are included in this book. Their backgrounds, ages, native intelligence, and emotional makeup are as varied as snowflakes. Yet, all of them have one thing in common—each found his or her best boss.

This book is not an encyclopedia. It will not lead you to the Dr. Spocklike solution. You can be taught to change a diaper without knowing much about yourself. You need only know how the diaper folds and how the baby doesn't. Changing your entrepreneurial attitude requires some introspection and some understanding of your own attitudes and those you want to have. However, after you have read the entire book, you will see how easy it is to use as a reference guide to remind you what you already know.

Countless courses and books are available to teach you how

your business should run. They can be very helpful if you remember that, no matter what they are called or how they are described, they teach you how your business—not you—should be run. There is a difference. Let me use my grandfather's business as an example. My grandfather didn't build railroads, start airlines, or begin a chain of restaurants, but he was an entrepreneur. Today he'd be called a recycler of vintage collectibles. He purchased or collected people's discards, which he then resold to a junk yard. My grandfather's business was his wagon and what went in and out of it, but the wagon went nowhere without the horse. Think of your business—no matter what kind it is—as a wagon and of yourself as the horse that pulls it. Although "point of information" sections offer some tips on how to maintain or operate your wagon, that is not this book's principal objective. The goal here is to teach you how to train and care for your horse, and you are the horse. So, if you wish, take those courses and read the books that teach you how to improve your wagon, but, first, improve the horse.

Some of the busiest and most successful people in our country agreed to be interviewed for this book. They gave of their valuable time because they think it is important for you to learn how to become an entrepreneur. Their fascinating and inspiring stories and lives are invaluable as examples. However, many of my clients, with whom I shared the trials and triumphs of being or becoming entrepreneurs, didn't know their experiences would be shared with you. Because some of my clients prefer anonymity, certain names have been changed and marked with an asterisk (*).

Lloyd E. Shefsky

Acknowledgments

Writing a book has proved my biggest challenge to date. When the labor seemed endless and the prospects bleak, nothing mattered more than encouragement from those I respected: Dean Don Jacobs, Professor Mort Kamien, Professor Norman Sigband, Professor Paul Rubenstein, Barbara Hendra, Robert Metz, and Jackie Landaw.

As a child, I learned to appreciate the magic of writing from my mother, Esther Shefsky, who writes beautifully and encouraged me to strive. And I learned from the example of my father, Sam Shefsky, that entrepreneurs are a special breed who grow through trials and tribulations as well as successes.

This book became an entrepreneurial project for me, and its allure could have become all-consuming. Fortunately, my lovely wife, Natalie, who has helped in numerous ways, continually reminded me to stop and smell the roses. I hope this book helps you become an entrepreneur and that you too are blessed with such beautiful ballast.

As with any entrepreneurial project, many redrafts were necessary. My thanks to the many typists who helped me, and especially to Diane Weber and Gail Leicht, who carried the brunt of that burden. My appreciation also to my assistant, Helen Michels, who handled the contacts and appointments with interviewees and others. And no entrepreneurial project can succeed without a marketing plan and effort. Mine was assisted by Barbara Hendra, Barry Merkin, George Goldberg, and Laura Friedman, Cynthia Borg, Debbie Innie, and Kathy Gilligan, the last four of McGraw-Hill, as well as the many friends and relatives who volunteered, often not knowing what that entailed, for which I am touched and thankful.

Caroline Carney was my editor at McGraw-Hill. Her energy was exceeded only by her capability. And her background in marketing further enhanced her talents as an editor. Most of all, her sensitivity and reasonableness made the process enjoyable, an unexpected bonus.

My clients, almost all entrepreneurs, have been my teachers, while providing me the joy of helping them. And my partners at the Chicago firm of Shefsky & Froelich Ltd. have been tolerant and generous in their support. But this book would have been impossible were it not for the hundreds of entrepreneurs who took time from the busiest of schedules to share their extraordinary insight. To them, giving back is as important as achieving.

The following list is a tribute to their talent, their traits, and their generosity:

Larry H. Adler, founder, Adler Development, Inc.

James Alexander, high school counselor

Raphael H. Amit, Ph.D., University of British Columbia

Ellen Anderson, Clairol Mentor Program, Clairol Corporation

Efraim Arazi, founder, Scitex; founder, Electronics for Imaging, Inc.

Mary Kay Ash, founder, Mary Kay Cosmetics

John Baratta, staff director, McDonald's Corporation

Sydney Biddle Barrows, author of *Mayflower Madam* and *Mayflower Manners*; founder, Cachet

Edward R. Beauvais, founder, America West Airlines

James A. Belasco, Ph.D., founder, Management Development Associates; author, *Teaching the Elephant to Dance*; publisher, *The Elephant Newsletter*

Peter Bensinger, founder, Bensinger, Dupont & Associates, Inc.; former director, U.S. Drug Enforcement Agency

Terri Bentz, founder, Terri Bentz, Inc. (wedding gown designer)

Devon Blaine, founder, The Blaine Group, Inc.; and former actress on "The Beverly Hillbillies" TV show

Donald Boroian, president and founder, Francorp, Inc.

Steven Brill, founder, Courtroom Television Network; founder, *The National Law Journal*

Charles Bronfman, cochair of the Board, The Seagram Company, Ltd.; founder, Montreal Expos baseball team

Robert Buckwald, Ph.D., president, CI Systems, Inc.

Richard Buskirk, Ph.D., former chairman, Entrepreneurship Department, University of Southern California

Dan Carroll, founder, The Carroll Group, Inc.; former chairman, Booz, Allen, Hamilton; former president, Gould, Inc.; former president, Hoover Universal, Inc.; director of numerous public corporations

Christopher Cerf, founder, Christopher Cerf Associates; coauthor, *Official Politically Correct Dictionary & Handbook*; producer, writer, composer, and humorist

Otto Clark, founder, Clark Copy International Corp.

Dr. James B. Cloonan, founder, American Association of Individual Investors

Sheila Cluff, founder, Sheila's Spas—The Palms at Palm Springs and The Oaks at Ojai in California

Ben Cohen, cofounder, Ben & Jerry's Ice Cream

Burt Cohen, vice president, McDonald's Corporation, Franchisee Selection Department

Howard Cohen, president, Operation Independence

James Covert, founder, SecurityLink; former U.S. Secret Service agent (protecting three presidents)

Jenny Craig, founder, Jenny Craig International

Gertrude Ramsay Crain, chairwoman of the Board, Crain Communications, Inc.

Lester Crown, chairman of the board, Material Service Corporation

Haim Dabah, founder, Gitano Group, Inc.

James Daverman, founder, Marquette Venture Partners

Edson de Castro, founder, Data General Corporation

Michael Dell, founder, Dell Computer Corporation

John Dickinson, former CEO, Junior Achievements

Henry Dorfman, founder, Thorn Apple Valley

Evelyn Echols, founder, The Echols Travel & Hotel Schools

Robert Engelman, founder, University Financial Corporation

William F. Farley, founder, Farley Industries

Sybil Ferguson, founder, Diet Center

Debbi Fields, founder, Mrs. Fields, Inc.

Andrew Filipowski, founder, Platinum Technologies, Inc.

Lee Flaherty, founder, Flair Communications Agency

Eileen Ford, founder, Ford Model Agency

Diane Freis, founder, Diane Freis International

Art Fry, Intrapreneur, 3M Company; inventor of Post-it Notes

Robert Galvin, chairman, Motorola, Inc.

Steve Garvey, founder, Garvey Marketing Group; former San Diego Padres baseball All-Star

Harold Geneen, former chief executive officer of ITT (highest-paid U.S. executive for 10 consecutive years); presently an entrepreneur

Sue Ling Gin, founder, Flying Food Fare Inc.

Stan Golder, founder, Golder, Thoma & Cressey

Bernard A. Goldhirsh, founder and chairman, *Inc.* magazine

Philip Goldman, founder, Pizza Now! Inc.

Ellen R. Gordon, president, Tootsie Roll Industries, Inc.

Gary Greenberg, cofounder, Sage Enterprises, Inc.

Jack Greenberg, vice chairman and chief financial officer, McDonald's Corporation

Jerry Greenfield, cofounder, Ben & Jerry's Ice Cream

Carl Haas, founder, Carl Haas Import Motors; cofounder, Paul Newman Racing Team

W. Van Harlow, III, professor, The University of Arizona

Christine Hefner, vice chairperson, president, chief operating officer, Playboy Enterprises, Inc.

Ned Heizer, founder, Heizer Corporation; previously headed Allstate Venture Capital

Milton Herzog, former superintendent, Stevenson High School, Prairie View, Illinois

Gerald E. Hill, Denton Thorne Professor of Entrepreneurship, University of Illinois at Chicago

Don Hindman, owner, Clark Foodservice, Inc.; founder, Time Container

Leslie Hindman, founder, Leslie Hindman Antiques

Raymond Hung, founder, Applied International Holdings Ltd., Hong Kong; Quorum International Inc., Phoenix, Arizona

Holly Hunt, founder, Holly Hunt, Ltd.

Suzanne Isaacs, founder, SVE/Society for Visual Education, Inc.

Mary Anne Jackson, founder, My Own Meals, Inc.

Victoria B. Jackson, president and owner, Diesel Sales and Service and Prodiesel, Inc.

Donald P. Jacobs, dean, Kellogg School of Management, Northwestern University

Helmut Jahn, head of Murphy/Jahn, Inc.

Jay Jenkins, public school teacher

George E. Johnson, founder, Johnson Products Company, Inc. (the first black-managed public corporation in the United States)

George Kalidonis, president, Technology Planning and Development; managing general partner, Chicago Capital Fund

Morton Kamien, Ph.D., professor of entrepreneurship, Kellogg School of Management, Northwestern University

Ross Kapstein, Atlanta middle school teacher

Dennis Keller, founder, Keller Schools—now DeVry Institute

Joseph Kellman, founder, Globe Glass & Mirror; founder (with other top executives), The Corporate School, Chicago, Illinois

Helen Klecka, mother of entrepreneur

The Honorable Philip Klutznick, former U.S. Secretary of Commerce; founder, Urban Investment & Development Company

Margie Korshak, founder, Margie Korshak Public Relations Firm

Marilyn Kourilsky, Ph.D., vice president of the Ewing Marion Kauffman Foundation's Center for Entrepreneurial Leadership

Otto Kroeger, founder, Otto Kroeger Associates; coauthor, *Type Talk*

Samuel J. LeFrak, chairman, The LeFrak Organization (owns 100,000 New York apartment units); founder of numerous businesses

Sherren Leigh, founder and publisher, Leigh Communications (*Today's Chicago Woman*)

Ian Leopold, founder, Campus Concepts; founder, Entrepreneur Club, Kellogg School, Northwestern University

Joe Levy, founder, numerous car agencies; sponsor, Entrepreneurship Chair, Kellogg School, Northwestern University

Larry Levy, founder and chairman, The Levy Restaurants (Spiaggia, Bistro 110, and The Blackhawk Lodge—Chicago; The Dive—Los Angeles and Las Vegas; Portobello Yacht Club and The Fireworks Factory—Orlando)

James Liautaud, founder, K-40 Electronics

Arthur Lipper, III, former chairman/editor, *Venture Magazine*

Paul Loeb, founder, American Backhaulers

Edward Lowe, founder, Edward Lowe Industries (kitty litter)

Sid Luckman, all-time great quarterback of the "Monsters of the Midway" Chicago Bears; partner, Cellu-Craft Midwest Inc.

John MacDowell, former president, Joint Council on Economic Education

Judd Malkin, cofounder, JMB Realty

Joseph R. Mancuso, founder, The Center for Entrepreneurial Management, Inc.

William Massey, vice president, Finance, Stanford University

Phillip Matthews, owner and president, Bell Sports

Richard Melman, founder, Lettuce Entertain You (owner of over 30 successful restaurants)

Barry Merkin, professor of entrepreneurship, Kellogg School, Northwestern University; former vice president and general merchandise manager, Walden Books

Sam Metzger, cofounder, Chipwich, Inc.

Stuart L. Meyer, Ph.D., professor of entrepreneurship, Kellogg School, Northwestern University

Marilyn Miglin, founder, Marilyn Miglin Inc. (manufacturer of fine cosmetics and perfumes; creator of "Destiny" and "Pheremone" fragrance lines); former Chez Paree Adorable and dancer in Jimmy Durante's troupe

Jack Miller, founder, Quill Corporation; cofounder (with school superintendent) of entrepreneurship awareness program

Elaine Moseley, Ph.D., principal, Corporate/Community Schools of America

Rebecca Mueller, New Business Development Department, NutraSweet Company

Phyllis C. Myers, Ph.D., executive director, One-to-One Learning Center

Burt Nanus, Ph.D., professor, Department of Management, School of Business, University of Southern California; coauthor, *Leaders: The Strategies for Taking Charge*

Judith Niedermaier, founder, Niedermaier, Inc.

James Nordstrom, cochairman, Nordstrom's Department Stores

Ike Pappas, founder, Ike Pappas Network Productions, Inc.; former CBS correspondent

James Paradiso, director, Center for Entrepreneurship, National-Lewis University

Patricia Pike, public school teacher

Barry Potekin, founder, Gold Coast Dogs chain; winner, *Inc.*/Ernst & Young Entrepreneur of the Year Award, 1988

Jay Pritzker, founder, Hyatt Hotels

Jerry Reinsdorf, founder, The Balcor Company; current owner of the Chicago White Sox and the Chicago Bulls

Jack Reynolds, founder, Jack Reynolds Communications; former NBC correspondent

Patrick Reynolds, founder, Reynolds Goodwin Corporation (program to help end smoking habits); grandson of R. J. Reynolds

Bernard B. Rinella, Chicago's best-known divorce lawyer

Shari Ring, founder, Occasions

Thurman John Rodgers, founder, Cypress Semiconductor Corp.

Jerry Rogers, founder, Cyrix Corp.

John W. Rogers, Jr., founder, Ariel Capital Management, Inc.

Philip Rollhaus, founder, Quixote Corporation

Philip J. Romano, founder, Fuddruckers; founder, Romano's Macaroni Grill

Pamela Rose, founder, Rose & Associates Office Group, Inc.

Gary Rosenberg, founder, UDC Homes, Inc.

Alan Rosenfeld, public school teacher

Howard Ruff, founder, The Ruff Company and *The Ruff Times*; formerly, regional franchisee of Evelyn Wood Reading Dynamics

Patrick G. Ryan, founder, Aon Corporation

Antoinette Saunders, Ph.D., founder, Stress Education Center for Children and Families

Terry Savage, former CBS financial reporter; author, *Terry Savage Talks Money: The Common-Sense Guide to Money Matters* and *Terry Savage's New Money Strategies for the 90's*

Howard Schultz, founder, Starbucks Coffee

Gordon Segal, founder, Crate & Barrel

Joe Segel, founder, The Franklin Mint; founder, QVC

Eyal Shavit, founder, Manof; cofounder, Office Channel; cofounder, TSA Associates

Isadore Sharp, founder, Four Seasons Hotels, Inc.

Peter J. Shea, chairman of the board and chief executive officer, Entrepreneur Group (*Entrepreneur* Magazine)

Walter Shorenstein, founder, Shorenstein Co.

Norman B. Sigband, Ph.D., former chairman, Department of Communications, School of Business, University of Southern California; author, *Communications for Management and Business* and *Business Communications*

Frederick W. Smith, founder, Federal Express

Dr. Michael Smurfit, chairman of the Board, Jefferson Smurfit Group Ltd., Ireland

Harry Snow, founder, Snow Aviation International, Inc.

E. Roe Stamps, IV, founder, Summit Partners

W. R. "Witt" Stephens, founder, Stephens Inc. (firm that took Wal-Mart and Tyson public; ranked thirteenth among investment banking firms in the United States)

Joe Sullivan, founder, Sullivan & Proops; former president, Swift & Company

Les Teichner, founder, The Chicago Group; cofounder, TSA Associates

Dan Tolkowsky, founder, Athena Fund; premier venture capitalist of Israel; former head of Israel Air Force

Jovan Trboyevic, founder, Jovan's, Le Perroquet, and Club Les Nomades

Lillian Vernon, founder, Lillian Vernon Corporation

Alice Walton, founder, Llama Asset Management Company; daughter of Sam Walton (founder of Wal-Mart Stores, Inc.)

Gail Ward, director, Disney School—participant in Junior Achievement programs

John L. Ward, professor, Loyola University; cofounder, *Family Business Review* and The Family Firm Institute

Joan Weinstein, founder, Ultimo, Ltd., Sonia Rykiel, Jil Sander, and Giorgio Armani (four Chicago high-fashion boutiques)

Harold P. Welsch, Ph.D., professor of entrepreneurship, DePaul University; founder, International Council for Small Business

Stef Wertheimer, founder, Iscar, Ltd.

Elmer L. Winter, cofounder, Manpower, Inc.

E. Katherine Wood, director of awards, Freedom Foundation at Valley Forge

Sam Zell, founder, Equity Financial Management Company; owner, Itel Corporation, Great Lakes International, and Great American Management and Investment; organized the Merrill Lynch "Gravedancers" fund, called Zell/Merrill Lynch Real Estate Opportunity Partners

This list excludes certain entrepreneurs who requested anonymity as well as clients of my firm whose circumstances make confidentiality mandatory.

In my professional practice, I deal with clients on a one-on-one basis, enabling me to be specific and concrete. Of necessity, a book such as this is aimed at a generic audience. But there is nothing generic about an entrepreneur. So, if you have particular questions about your future as an entrepreneur, drop me a line:

Lloyd E. Shefsky
Shefsky & Froelich Ltd.
444 N. Michigan Avenue
Chicago, Illinois 60611
Fax: 312-527-4011

1

A Simple Way to Understand Entrepreneurship

In a time of turbulence and change, it is more true than ever that knowledge is power.
PRESIDENT JOHN FITZGERALD KENNEDY

When you ask people what they do for a living, don't you react differently to the following response: "I manage a chain of four stores," than you do to a person who says, "The business I started and own now consists of four stores"? I'll bet you do. Almost everyone finds entrepreneurs exciting for several reasons:

1. *Entrepreneurs are the prototype of the American persona.* Unlike managers (no matter how successful they may be), entrepreneurs have an added dimension. Just having the determination to follow their dreams entitles them to respect and admiration and makes them the envy of those who thought about it but "chickened out." Entrepreneurs are accorded almost as much respect as patriots and heroes; they are, after all, the prototype of the American persona. Ask foreigners to describe a typical American businessperson, and they will portray an entrepreneur.

2. *Businesses, meet your creator.* There is something godlike about creativity, and entrepreneurs are creators. Managers create profits only from existing businesses (a valuable function but by no means godly). Entrepreneurs aren't omnipotent, but their ability to create a business where none existed is reason for respect, even awe.

3. *Entrepreneurial passion is catching.* Entrepreneurs are passionate about their business dream, and they transmit their passion to others. That's how entrepreneurs make things happen. The passion that prompts them to take risks and make their dreams become reality infects and attracts others to jump on their bandwagon.

    Entrepreneurs can't contain themselves; they promote their businesses continually, even when they aren't actively selling. They are like proud parents showing off their baby's pictures. You may not care about their particular baby, but their passion about it and the miracle of its birth may infect you.

4. *Entrepreneurs are the Sinatras of business.* If you are an entrepreneur, you get to do it your way. Frank Sinatra's hit song, "My Way," wasn't a big hit just because of Sinatra's great voice and delivery. He sold the song by embodying its spirit in his lifestyle. People enjoyed—perhaps even envied—Sinatra, as he boldly proclaimed that he did things his way and loved it. We feel the same way about entrepreneurs. We respect and admire entrepreneurs for marching to their own tune, which isn't "Nine to Five."

Forget Your Ancestors; Your Descendants Are What Matter

If you don't understand what an entrepreneur is and how to become one, the act of selecting yourself as your boss may be premature and could leave you unemployed. However, properly prepared, you can pick your best boss and join an elite club—the Society of Entrepreneurs. Joining is easy. To pledge yourself to the Society's principles and goals, you must learn what they are about. The aim of this book is to show you. The Society's hazing is self-imposed. Only you decide whether you will be accepted as a member.

"Entrepreneur" may connote the American Dream, but in the United States, you aren't born to that title of respect, and the Queen doesn't bestow it with a sword on your shoulder. Entrepreneurs are common people, of varying capabilities and talents, who have learned certain traits. I can teach you to develop those same characteristics so you can pick your best boss and become an entrepreneur.

Perhaps you're concerned that being entrepreneurial isn't an acquired talent; either you've got it or you won't ever get it. Thurman J. Rodgers, who founded Cypress Semiconductor, one of the best and most profitable silicone chip companies, responds this way to people who ask him whether they should become an entrepreneur: "If you don't already know that, then the answer is 'no' or, at least, 'you shouldn't be asking me.'" Rodgers is saying that such people are not asking the wrong question, they are asking the wrong person. He knows that there is much to learn and you should ask questions. But, ask them of yourself. This book will help you raise and answer the right questions.

You won't see Bill Gates' picture on a Wheaties box, but just like Wheaties champions, entrepreneurs are made not born. Like champions, they are self-made. But even champion athletes have coaches. Through this book, I'll be your coach. I can coach you, but you'll have to practice entrepreneurial calisthenics.

Emulate; Don't Idolize

Entrepreneurs can rise to positions of national power, prestige, wealth, fame, and acclaim. Magazine covers and TV shows feature entrepreneurs such as Debbi Fields of Mrs. Fields Cookies, Stephen Jobs of Apple Computer, Hugh Hefner of *Playboy*, and Ross Perot who founded EDS and sold it to General Motors for $1 billion. Who would have dreamed that an entrepreneur could reshape the U.S. political system and, at the same time, help topple a sitting President? Equally impressive is William Gates, who started Microsoft and achieved a net worth of over a billion dollars while still in his early twenties. These are a few of the giants, the entrepreneurial legends.

Do you idolize successful entrepreneurs and wonder if you can measure up to them? Is that how you feel? If you do, your perspective may be wrong. The legendary entrepreneurs start out with the same basic characteristics as everyone else. Some may be smarter, more charismatic, or plain luckier than others; that's why everyone can't make their entrepreneurship legendary. But it's not necessary to become a legend to be a successful entrepreneur.

Many Major League baseball players today earn millions of dollars a year doing what they love but will never make it into the Baseball Hall of Fame. In the same way, tens of thousands of entrepreneurs are extremely successful and professionally satisfied, but few will ever appear on the covers of *Inc.* or *Fortune*, ever be the guest or subject on a network TV show, or receive a White House call for advice. They are content just the same.

The local baker with a single small store does not start out much differently than Debbi Fields, who founded Mrs. Fields Cookies, or than Charlie Lubin, who referred to himself as "the little old baker," forgot about his ancestors, and named his company after his daughter, Sara Lee. Their businesses may grow larger and more successful, but they all put on their entrepreneurial pants one leg at a time and are not any more entrepreneurial than you can be. To be an entrepreneur, you don't have to be:

- A genius
- A hotshot
- An MBA
- Wealthy

You must want to be an entrepreneur. You must want it very much. If you do and if you follow my advice, becoming an entrepreneur will be relatively easy. Before you know it, you'll be your own boss.

What Is an Entrepreneur?

Dictionary definitions of *entrepreneur* are useless. All of us may believe that we can spot one when we see one, but how do we describe what an entrepreneur is? I define *entrepreneur* by taking the three parts of the word: *entre, pre,* and *neur,* and tracing them to their Latin roots: *entre* means enter; *pre* means before; and *neur* means nerve center. I define an entrepreneur as someone who enters a business—any business—in time to form or change substantially that business's nerve center.

My definition isn't concerned with whether people start their businesses, buy them, inherit them, win them in a poker game, gain control of them in a proxy fight, or even own them. It doesn't matter whether the business is a fledgling start-up or an institutional giant. All that matters is that individuals develop or change the nerve center of the business. Those individuals are entrepreneurs.

Preparation Eases the Stretch for the Brass Ring

There are many different types of business opportunities, but, unfortunately, opportunities alone do not create an entrepreneur. Marilyn Miglin, whose cosmetics business manufactures "Destiny" and "Pheromone" perfumes, recalls the words of her dance teacher, "Success is when opportunity meets preparation." That opportunity can be simple luck—you happen to be in the right place at the right time—or you may even create your own opportunities with preparation. However opportunity and preparation meet, you must be ready to take advantage if you want to control your destiny and be an entrepreneur.

Peter Shea, who publishes *Entrepreneur Magazine,* remembers the advice of his stepfather: "Everybody gets at least one chance to grab the brass ring. The idea is to be intelligent enough to be in position to grasp the chance and go after it." I agree but believe that brass rings can be turned to gold by your being willing and ready to make your own special dream come true.

Perhaps you still feel you don't measure up. What do you think you lack? What's the most important characteristic you need to become an entrepreneur? Are you worried about the risk inherent in reaching for that opportunity?

Most people—even most entrepreneurs—believe that entrepreneurship is about having the courage to assume risks. Entrepreneurs are generally perceived as "bet the ranch," "got a hunch, risk a bunch," "go for it at any cost" types. They are assumed to have more nerve than professional gamblers because gamblers, at least, know the odds up front. What professional gambler would assume 9-to-1 odds against success? Yet, we continue to believe entrepreneurs welcome such odds since, according to published reports, 90 percent of all new businesses eventually fail.

If you buy the perceived wisdom—if you believe that being an entrepreneur is more risky than being a gambler—then you would have to be crazy to want to become an entrepreneur. I'm here to tell you that those assumptions are wrong:

- Entrepreneurship is not about courage or risks; it's about dreams.
- Entrepreneurs need not be gamblers.
- Your odds of succeeding as an entrepreneur can be favorable, if you prepare yourself.

Everyone in any endeavor takes on some risks and reaps some rewards. Don't assume that entrepreneurs encounter more of both than other people do. Knowing how much certain people put at risk and how big their potential reward may be tells me only how shrewdly they negotiate their deals. Such knowledge reveals nothing to me about whether those people are entrepreneurs.

It's not that entrepreneurs take more risk, although some do, but that they focus on the opportunity, have confidence in their dream and in their ability to make it happen, and see their alternatives as less exciting, less fulfilling, and dismal.

At age 28, Efi Arazi founded Scitex, an Israeli company whose equipment immediately revolutionized the printing industry's use of color pictures and now prepares the covers of magazines such as *Time*. Efi Arazi told me that, at the time, he saw no risks because his alternative was "being consigned to a grey life as a peon in an organization that measures your contribution by longevity not ability, which to me was death."

Rejection: Your Invitation to Be a Somebody

Respect and success—everyone wants that. Margie Korshak's father is a well-known Chicago politician. She started her own public relations firm, she told me, "because I wanted to be a somebody, like my father was." Do you dream about being "a somebody"? As Jane Wagner said in *The Search for Intelligent Life in the Universe*, the show she wrote for her friend, Lily Tomlin: "I always wanted to be a somebody. Then I realized I had to get more specific." Before you can imagine being successful and respected as an entrepreneur, you have to think about becoming one, as did Margie Korshak and the hundreds of other entrepreneurs I've interviewed and represented.

If risk taking and other such characteristics are not relevant, what is? How can you know how to be a specific somebody when you haven't figured out what kind of somebody you want to be? Without having been there before, how can you envision what you aspire to be? The answer is to learn from those who have already done it.

Imagine with me for a moment. You come up with a great idea—a new gizmo that everyone would want, a new service that everyone needs, or a new way to do a job better. You go to your boss and share your great idea with her. She says the company wants no part of it. You start to realize that you have the wrong boss. You then approach your father, your rich uncle, and even your beloved grandmother for backing. They all tell you your idea is silly and that you don't have the experience to pull it off, or, worse yet, they laugh. That can be very demoralizing. After all, you didn't approach just anyone. You selected people whom you respect, and they are the very ones who tell you that you're wrong and that your dream is impossible.

In the 1950s, Ray Kroc approached every one of his relatives, friends, and acquaintances for backing to buy a new kind of hamburger drive-in restaurant. Most of them thought his idea ridiculous and advised him to stick to selling milk shake blenders. From time to time, Ray Kroc may have been discouraged, but he was never deterred. Instead, he forged ahead. Eventually, he acquired his funding, bought a successful hamburger stand named McDonald's, and changed the complexion of drive-in restaurants and the landscape of the world. Today, Kroc may seem bigger than life, but once he was not. He was simply a milk shake blender salesman who realized that the McDonald's format could be refined and cloned worldwide. If Kroc could succeed, so can you.

Scenarios of rejection occur thousands of times each day in the United States, but they don't have to happen to you. More than 600,000 times a year an American starts a new business. Each and every one of them probably had to overcome rejection. You don't have to be Ray Kroc to overcome rejection, but it may help you to know how some entrepreneurs did overcome it.

Famous, successful entrepreneurs may seem immune to the barriers that confront you. However, like you, many of them once worked for big companies and had intimidating bosses. Dr. Ed Land founded Polaroid when his boss at Kodak wasn't interested in his concept for an instant camera. When IBM wanted no part of the computer service opportunity Ross Perot saw, Perot formed EDS. Years later, he sold the company to General Motors for $1 billion. Hugh Hefner asked his boss at *Esquire Magazine* for a raise. If his salary had been increased $5 a week, Hefner might have stayed, *Playboy* might never have been founded, and bunnies would be known only for their big ears. When you are an entrepreneur you negotiate your salary while looking in a mirror. Think about it.

Kroc, Land, Perot, and Hefner each had gigantic dreams. Sure, they were exceptionally talented! That's why they made hundreds of millions. You may not achieve their success, but would you settle for millions instead of billions—at least for starters? Then study where they came from and how they got somewhere.

2
Begin with a Dream

Nothing happens unless first a dream.
CARL SANDBURG

The most dramatic events in world history were motivated by dreams. The exodus of Hebrew slaves from Egypt succeeded because Moses, heavenly inspired, dreamed that his people could be free. The American Revolution was the result of people's dreams of freedom, democracy, and justice. Martin Luther King galvanized his people with his speech, "I Have a Dream."

Entrepreneurs, too, have worked tirelessly pursuing their dreams: Henry Ford dreamed of a car that everyone could afford. Stephen Jobs dreamed of a user-friendly computer; Charlie Lubin dreamed of a cheese cake that nobody doesn't like; Edwin Land dreamed of a company built around an instant camera; and Ray Kroc dreamed about selling billions of hamburgers.

Now, you know what it takes to begin. All you need is a dream.

A Special Kind of Dream

Would-be entrepreneurs live in a sea of dreams. Their destinations are private islands—places to build, create, and transform their particular dreams into reality. Being an entrepreneur entails envisioning your island, and even more important, it means getting in the boat and rowing to your island. Some leave the shore and drift aimlessly in the shallow waters close to shore, while others paddle furiously and get nowhere, because they don't know how to paddle or steer. Worst of all are those who remain on the shore of the mainland, afraid to get in the boat. Yet, all those dreamers may one day be entrepreneurs if they can marshal the resources—external and internal—needed to transform their dreams into reality.

Everyone has dreams. We all dream while asleep, even if we don't remember dreaming. Entrepreneurs' dreams are different. Their dreams are not limited to dreams about fantasy islands or fast cars. Theirs are about business. The two kinds of dreams sometimes merge. They did for such entrepreneurs as Chris Hemmeter (the developer of tropical resorts and casino hotels) and Ferdinand Porsche (the founder of Porsche Car).

Entrepreneurs dream not just about becoming independent but also about a particular product or service, method of distribution or manufacture, or new form of marketing or selling. And they are willing to do what it takes to make that dream real, as long as they do it while working for the best bosses possible—themselves. Both elements—the business and the ability to determine your own destiny—must be present if the dream is to be an entrepreneurial dream.

The entrepreneur's dream is different in another respect too. This dream visualizes a long-term goal and its realization. Jerry Rogers is the founder of Cyrix, a manufacturer of microprocessor chips whose early results caused analysts to refer to it as "one of the more dramatic start-up companies in the semiconductor business." Rogers notes that "80 percent of what you do is drudgery and 20 percent is fun. Don't get hung up," he advises, "on what you are doing today. Look far enough out that you get the satisfaction that you are making headway toward that end goal." Defining the dream so it encompasses long-term goals yet includes a clear path to the dream's realization makes it that special kind of dream.

Prospectuses, business plans, and loan applications describe business opportunities, but they cannot describe the dream. An entrepreneur's dream of a business opportunity is like a painting; no one can discern a painting's quality or value in the dark. Similarly, a business opportunity is lifeless and invisible until the entrepreneur's dream sheds light on the opportunity and illuminates its possibilities. If the dream is bright enough, then the opportunity can become a reality.

You may still be dreaming about fantasy islands or fast cars. That's okay. You've mastered the hard part; you're dreaming. Now change the subject matter of your dream.

I See It; Why Can't You?

If you are not the most creative person in the world, don't worry. The dream is in the eyes of the beholder, not exclusively in those of the creator. Many business dreams are not conceived by the entrepreneur; often they are adoptions of someone else's dream. Jerry Greenfield, one of the founders of Ben & Jerry's Ice Cream, is most certainly an entrepreneur, even though Jerry confessed to me that the dream was Ben's. Jerry adopted Ben's dream; then, with Ben, they made it a reality. So, even if it's not your dream, by adopting the dream and committing yourself to making it a reality, it becomes your dream too.

I remember a client, Marvin Packard*, who had built a small food purveying business to sales of approximately $4 million. Marvin made a good living, providing for his children's tuition at three top colleges and two graduate schools, membership at a luxurious club, two European cars, and a lovely house. Marvin lived well, but at his country club, where many members measured their net worth in tens of millions, Marvin was a small fry.

One day, one of these much wealthier country club members struck up a conversation with Marvin. It seems that Mr. Big Bucks and a few of his well-heeled pals were considering a new venture and wanted Marvin to join them. He knew they had invited him because of his knowledge in an area that was foreign to them. The venture they contemplated entailed selling to chains in many markets. It was gigantic—far beyond the scope of Marvin's enterprise. Alone, Marvin wouldn't have had the nerve to dream so boldly, even though he knew he could make the venture succeed. But by being invited into the group, he felt honored; it boosted his self-esteem.

Actually, Mr. Big Bucks and his friends were smart to invite Marvin. At their very first meeting, Marvin saw a somewhat different and much more aggressive and dynamic dream than they had conceived. They agreed to adopt Marvin's dream and make it the new goal. The result was a huge success—a success far greater than Marvin's own business. Marvin told me that he was amazed. As he put it, "Here I am, a little pisher (small fry), whose dream was bigger than life. And all those big shots bought my dream."

Sharing a dream is a lot like offering to share half a glass of water with someone. You may see it as half full, while he sees it as half empty. The value of some of the world's most lucrative dreams has not been apparent to many who have been offered it. For that reason, most South and Central Americans speak Spanish, not Italian. Italian royalty couldn't see the value of Christopher Columbus's dream, whereas Spain's Queen Isabella could.

Whether a person can see someone else's dream is a function of the listener's ability to receive it as much as the dreamer's sales ability. Steven Brill founded *The American Lawyer,* a gossipy newspaper for larger law firms, and, more recently, Court TV, the cable network that covered the William Kennedy Smith and Mike Tyson rape trials. He told me he was convinced he could sell his dream to advertisers or anybody, because he believed in what he was doing, because he had bought his dream. Brill was so convinced that it took him "no time at all" to sell the concept of Court TV to the late Steve Ross, then the CEO of Time Warner, who helped Brill launch the business. Of course, in Ross, Brill had the right listener.

Sometimes, even the best seller and receiver can't connect. In the 1950s, Ray Kroc conceived a dream of great value. He saw how the McDonald brothers had developed a new fast food restaurant, and he wanted to franchise the idea everywhere. He retained their name and called his company McDonald's. Ray gave a friend and former colleague, John Grab, an early opportunity to take half of McDonald's in return for a $50,000 investment. John had the money and later proved to be an excellent entrepreneur himself. Ray really tried to sell John on the ideas he had for his dream. He drove John out to a drive-in restaurant and said, "We'll change this; we'll do that; we'll add this; and we'll remove that." Even though Ray believed in his dream totally and was effusive in describing it, John said, "Ray, all you're doing is removing the carhops." With that, John rejected Ray's offer of half the dream that became McDonald's.

Phil Rollhaus is the founder of Quixote, a small but growing publicly held, diversified, high-technology company that makes highway crash cushions, stenographic shorthand machines (such as those used in courtrooms), laser-read optical disks, medical diagnostic instruments, and other products. Even though he was a successful entrepreneur in his own right, he didn't recognize the promise of another man's dreams. Many years ago, two acquaintances, Robert Parrish and Wayne Parrish, told Phil they saw a market for one monthly reference book that listed all the flights of all the domestic airlines. Phil told them that this was a "dumb idea, because all you have to do is make a local telephone call to any airline to get all the information you need." Phil couldn't see the dream that Robert and Wayne Parrish saw and is the first to tell you how fortunate they are to have ignored him. They bought their own dream which became the popular *Official Airline Guide*.

When Ed Lowe's father looked at his clay business, he saw clay. Ed looked and saw Kitty Litter. The concept wasn't Ed's discovery. His father already sold some of his clay to people who used it for their cats, but he didn't focus on that application. Ed bought the business from his father and built "Kitty Litter" into a generic word, right up there with Kleenex, Coke, and Levi's.

Thus not every dream that is visible to certain dreamers is visible to others. Eventually, Ray Kroc and the Parrishes obtained their seed capital from people who could see and share their dreams. John, who couldn't see Ray's dream, and Phil, who couldn't see the Parrishes' dream, each saw his own dream so clearly that he could share it with others. How many times have you asked yourself "Why didn't I think of that?" The world is full of great ideas that weren't conceived by you or any of the world's greatest entrepreneurs. Whether you understand or see the value in someone else's dream is irrelevant. All you must do is see your own and be willing to convert that dream to reality. Of course, you can't realize a dream—your own or one you adopt—unless you see it and buy it.

Point of Information

Angels and Allies

Hundreds of would-be entrepreneurs have left their dreams in what I call their "dream drawer" because they thought they didn't have the sources for capital to develop their ideas. Actually, they had many more sources than they realized, and many of those sources are available to you also.

It helps if you have a wealthy uncle or indulgent parents with cash to spare. Angels are better yet because you don't have to live with them if things go awry. Seeking entrepreneur role models often can lead you to an angel. Some invest to become part of the entrepreneurial experience again. It is to your advantage that as financiers, they are less sophisticated than more demanding venture capitalists.

Angels who invest in start-ups have a variety of additional motives. The angel may think your business glamorous even if it isn't, say, a TV series, a gambling joint in Las Vegas, or a piece of a Broadway show. Angels have other motivations. Sometimes, they have sold their dreams, and they want a piece of yours. Or they may want an entree with your customers. They even may be investing for the wrong reasons, but, so long as you are honest, listen to Woody Allen: "Take the money and run." Although understanding your angel's motives may help you entice angelic largesse, ultimately it is all about getting capital and giving your investors a monetary return.

Strategic partners, who can bring to the table, in addition to money, the missing components for creating or growing your business, could answer some of your prayers. I consider these alliances one of the best capital sources around. In addition to money, the partner generally provides some of the complementary components (expensive parts of R&D, facilities for beta site testing, market testing, and so on) that are either beyond your means or beyond the scope of your goals. The capital investment component of these alliances can entail the risk partner transferring funds for stock of the poor partner or for ownership in a joint venture business. Sometimes, the risk partner merely expends funds internally to accomplish its part as a strategic partner.

An example of the latter arrangement is Bob Buckwald, an expert in infrared technology and founder of CI Systems. Through an Israeli subsidiary, CI developed military industry applications which proved critical in Desert Storm. Bob rightfully "feared" that peace might break out in the world and sought nonmilitary diversification. He concluded that his infrared technology could be applied to the manufacture of computer chips—the vital step of measuring the temperature of the silicon chip during the manufacturing process. The cost savings would prove compelling.

CI was then such a little company that the silicon application was starting a new business, virtually a new beginning. What was missing was not only the capital to do research and development but an actual production line for experimentation, knowledge about silicon chips, insight into the marketplace and its needs, and channels of distribution. So Bob found a strategic partner (Applied Materials), a half-billion-dollar leader in chip production, who had all the above. While fulfilling the knowledge, facility, and distribution needs, the deal substantially reduced CI's capital needs and created instant credibility, enabling CI to raise the funds required to fulfill its end of the bargain and for much more.

Applied Materials lacked the infrared technological skill but could see the benefit of the product—perhaps even better than Bob could because the company was the ultimate customer for the device. So we're talking about someone with a strategic reason for getting involved. From CI's perspective, it obtained what it needed for that one (silicon) application, without diluting its ownership in other applications businesses, such as medical instruments, a new business which CI has recently entered.

Bet you never thought of a competitor as a potential strategic partner, but I've done lots of those deals. They are not easy to do. You have to protect confidentiality and your trade secrets, but once you have the appropriate clauses in place and have dealt effectively with other competitive factors, such a deal can be mutually beneficial.

Strategic alliances are more common than you think. They are formed constantly—many each day. They are difficult to quantify because they aren't always labeled as such. Frequently, the entrepreneur is focused on the result and structures the relationship only to that end. Besides, these alliances don't fit any particular mold. Use your imagination to spot a potential strategic partner. What do you need? Who has it? Who could best see the potential? Who needs the ultimate product or service? The opportunity in a good strategic alliance justifies the effort and, often, giving up a piece of the dream.

If your start-up relies on expensive equipment, you might consider a leasing arrangement. If the equipment is readily reusable, the manufacturer may lease it to you. If the equipment helps you sell a consumable, the supplier of that consumable may lease it to you, e.g., soft drink syrup companies providing fountain equipment to restaurants. If, however, the equipment is unique or not easily transferred and if your financial statements are below the threshold for traditional leasing arrangements, you might consider venture leasing. In that situation, a leasing company serves as your venture capitalist of sorts by using a lease to finance the equipment. In turn, the leasing company will charge you for the lease and take a piece of the business.

Sometimes suppliers will provide some capital. Let's say your company will create and mail a catalog to your customers. In exchange for a fee, paid in advance, or a loan, you might arrange to feature the supplier's merchandise, and, in the right circumstances, place the supplier's name and logo in a prominent spot. This, by the way, may work to the firm's advantage if it can book its "investment" as an advertising expense. Offering to use a firm's logo makes it easier to get its participation. In general, it takes less to get approval of an advertising expense item than an investment. The latter often requires approval of special committees, top management, or even a board of directors.

All businesses have one supplier in common, the phone company. Consider the Regional Bell companies. It isn't widely known, but these cash-rich companies have venture capital sidelines. The companies originally set up these sidelines to side-step restrictions on the kinds of business they can own outright. Recently, those restrictions have eased, and some little Bells, such as Ameritech, have willingly sacrificed their monopoly position to enable their diversification. Now especially, if you can convince them you have the right stuff, you may find that the phone company is a willing partner.

Is Your Dream Gold or Fool's Gold?

How can you know for sure whether your dream is viable? How do you know whether to go for it? Notice, this question is not whether you will succeed but whether your product, service, channel, or whatever is viable. You are trying to determine whether your dream is gold or fool's gold, not whether you can extract the gold, evade the desperados, get it to the bank, and convert it to money.

You can seek help in determining the viability of your dream. Hiring experts raises problems—expense, protection of your secret, etc. There is an easier way. Plan to go into a business you already know something about. Dreamers tend to dream about the exotic. After all, when you don't know much about the subject, you are less likely to raise the problems that douse the flame in your belly. Would-be entrepreneurs are well advised not to seek opposites because they know less about opposites. Although it is true that the opposite poles of magnets quite naturally attract, the goal of entrepreneurs is to be a magnate, not a "magnet."

Richie Melman, the founder of Lettuce Entertain You and owner of more than 30 successful restaurants, advises entrepreneurial "wannabes" to follow their hearts. In particular, he says they should "do what they know and love. Otherwise, they don't stand a chance, because they'll be competing against someone like me—someone who knows and loves what he does."

When Desire Precedes Passion

Some wannabes that come to me for advice have no idea what business—or even industry—they want to be in. All they know is that they want to be in their own business. They have a million reasons why they should be their own boss. Some of those reasons are valid; some not. However, these people lack a critical ingredient to being an entrepreneur: They don't have a dream. They desire to be an entrepreneur but lack the passion only a dream can give them. I tell those wannabes to keep their engines revved but to search among the things they know and love for a dream that will avoid a dead-end and put them on the highway to success.

Richie Melman's advice is important. He's telling you to pursue what you know and love. Otherwise, your entrepreneurial dream might turn out to be a fantasy, rather than an opportunity. Some people—such as inventors and scientists—can turn their fantasies into realities, but for most people, fantasies are more difficult to make real. Don't reject a dream just because it's your fantasy, but don't select a fantasy unless you are willing to undertake a harder, riskier effort and believe you can make it your reality.

Becoming a successful entrepreneur is much easier if you follow those dreams that you understand. Wanting to be your own boss is a dream of escape. To be an entrepreneur you must also dream of your destination.

If You Don't Buy Your Dream, You Can't Sell It

Ultimately, you'll have to sell your dream to others; that's part of being an entrepreneur. My rule is: *If you don't buy your dream, you can't sell it.* How do you buy your dream? Buying a dream involves two steps:

1. You must believe in the dream itself.
2. You must believe that you are capable of pulling it off.

Entrepreneurs don't have to start out with perfect dreams, but they must believe they can make them perfect. Notice that you only need to believe in your dream and capability, not be 100 percent certain of the outcome. Don't wait for certainty. There are no sure things in this field. No one issues insurance policies on entrepreneurial ventures. But do be sold on your dream. When it comes to your dream, you are your most important customer.

Though all entrepreneurs must take these two steps, each entrepreneur takes the steps in his or her own way. Some are very deliberate—analyzing all the pros and cons. Others negotiate the steps without a second thought, in a seemingly instinctive way. Both ways work. You must determine which is more comfortable for you.

Thurman Rodgers typifies the extreme of taking the deliberative approach. Upon graduating from Dartmouth, he headed to Stanford, never having heard of the Silicon Valley. He unloaded his U-Haul and suddenly found himself in the middle of the breeding ground for high-tech entrepreneurs. Rodgers caught the fever. He decided early that he needed to run his own business (escape). He also had the requisite dream (destination), which I refer to as a better silicon "mousetrap." But he lacked practical experience in the industry. He gave a lot of thought to how to gain that experience in a time frame that didn't snuff out his flame. In his case, the pros were readily apparent: he knew that in the long term he wasn't suited to working for someone else. The cons required greater deliberation. His conclusion was that the cons were only a function of timing. As a result of his deliberative process, he put off his dream and, after receiving his Ph.D., worked at American Microsystems and, later, Advanced Micro Devices, in order to gain the experience he would need to run his own business.

Mary Anne Jackson, a highly energetic processed foods entrepreneur who runs her own newly formed company, is another example of the deliberative approach. Before starting her own business, she had been employed by Beatrice Foods, where she gained experience in strategic planning, turnarounds, project management, new product development, and operations. During those years she studied what it takes to be a boss, and she concluded that she could be one as well as anyone else. When Beatrice let her go, she studied the marketplace to find a product and a business. She followed the course Richie Melman suggests—stick to an area you know and love—and concentrated her search in the food business. As a mother of three, she knew there was a need for foods especially prepared for kids, and so, after more market research, she launched My Own Meals.

As a model of the instinctive process, let me tell you about someone I met years ago. The man, who owned, created, and built the largest west coast marina south of Tampa with his own hands, was an 80-something-year-old man called "Pop." During negotiations to buy the marina, Pop and I stood surveying its massive structure, and I asked Pop how he did it all. After all, he wasn't an architect, an engineer, a landscaper, or a marine biologist; in fact, he had never attended high school. How did he manage to create this phenomenal marina which he conceived and built all on his own?

I'll never forget Pop saying to me, "Well, I just looked out and saw how it should be, and it was." It was that simple: He saw his dream, it was very real to him, and he believed he could pull it off. He may not have said all those things to himself at the time. He certainly didn't go through all the investigative, analytical, and deliberative thought processes that Thurman Rodgers and Mary Anne Jackson did, but Pop took the same two key steps all the same. He bought his dream, and believed he could pull it off, and by buying the dream he owned it.

Profile

Pop: The Twilight Years of a Blue-Collar Visionary

It isn't often that someone retires before becoming an entrepreneur, but it does happen. Colonel Sanders financed his first restaurant with his social security check, and, as you know, he went on to build the Kentucky Fried Chicken chain. Like Colonel Sanders, Pop was old enough that he didn't have to fire a boss. Pop was retired when he began staring at his ocean frontage on the Gulf of Mexico. He bought the undeveloped seashore property in the 1950s. His marina became, late in life, his baby, his child. This "fertile" retiree was to nurture his dream with as much TLC and anxiety as a much younger parent.

Pop not only had little education, his hands were hardened by manual labor. Pop didn't know the best way to build a marina. He clearly didn't know how to erect it the way a well-trained marine architect would, using state-of-the-art methods. Yet his marina was quite sound. It proved to be a first-class structure in every way. A marine architect might have used a foundation of steel-reinforced concrete struts for the six-story honeycomb of boat slips. Pop poured a solid concrete base. That may have cost more, but it probably cost a lot less than a college education in architecture. Anyway, it was too late for Pop to have that choice, and besides, the lack of education didn't stop Pop from making things happen.

Lack of education—a common antidote to many wannabes' entrepreneurial instincts—didn't stop Pop. Neither did the fact that most people his age were quietly retired. It is never too late to pursue a dream. And there's no SAT or IQ test for entrepreneurial dreamers.

Buying your dream is not as easy as seeing it, because buying means spending—spending energy, time, reputation, ego, and a host of other resources. Those costs cause some people to leave their dreams tucked safely away in their dream drawers. You must learn to measure that cost more precisely and less emotionally. There's not as much to lose as you may think. You must also learn how to use resources efficiently, so they pale when compared with what can be gained. What is easier than believing in your own dream? After all, you're not being asked to buy someone else's—only your own. Believing in your dream is a critical step toward making your dream a reality.

Point of Information

Your Backers and That Fast Shuffle: Pie on the Sly

It is very difficult for most entrepreneurs to raise money, so many raise all they can in one heroic effort. They figure everything will work out perfectly, and they'll only have to go to the well one time. Take my word for it, they are almost always wrong.

In the rush to attract capital, you may not take the time to consider carefully your long-term financial needs. Predicting how much you will need to open the door is easy; projecting how long you will take to break even and estimating how much capital you will need to cover that deficit are far more difficult. Some, in the enthusiasm of starting a business, sell themselves on rosy forecasts such as: "We're going to do great. We are going to meet our capital needs with the cash we put in the register. We won't need more outside money." But 99 percent of businesses do need additional capital somewhere down the road.

Smart entrepreneurs figure this out in advance. They curb their enthusiasm and coolly prepare projections of sales and breakeven points. Sure, more conservative projections may give a bigger up-front piece of the business to investors, but the difference may not be as big as you'll be forced to surrender in a desperate second phase capital raise. Cash in the bank should be the entrepreneur's equivalent of a "bird in the hand."

Entrepreneurial confidence and optimism must give way to objective reason. Suppose you go to a venture capitalist firm. You are eager to sell them, and they know it. Interested in making the best deal they can, they pretend they are convinced that you'll meet your business projections and that you won't need a second round of financing later on. But they are going to watch you like a hawk. And, if you don't meet the promised projections, even though it becomes clear that success is just around the corner, they are going to take a lot more equity than they would have taken had you been forthright and reasonable up front. In fact, their lawyer may insist on a clause in your initial contract, reducing your founder's shares if projections aren't met. When I represent the venture capitalist in a transaction, that's what I try to do.

So project conservatively. For if you don't make the numbers you project, the venture capitalist may take an extra slice of the equity pie on the sly...with or without forewarning. That slice will come out of *your* equity in the business.

3

Dream
Drawers

Good morning, Daddy!
Ain't you heard
The boogie-woogie rumble
Of a dream deferred?

LANGSTON HUGHES
Dream Boogie

Milton Herzog had a dream drawer. I met Milton Herzog when he was the superintendent of Stevenson High School in Lincolnshire, Illinois. He is a progressive and dedicated advocate of teaching high school students about the free enterprise system and entrepreneurship. With Jack Miller, the founder of Quill Corporation, Milt developed an interactive program that allowed students to learn about entrepreneurship first hand, by visiting Quill's factory and through hearing Jack talk about his work.

In the midst of our discussion on entrepreneurship, Milt opened his desk drawer, pulled out a business plan, and said, "This is my dream; it's a game called 'Zoggy Ball' and it could be a great hit. I wish someone would pick it up and run with it." Milt saw his dream but couldn't buy it. He wasn't prepared to take the plunge, and, as a result, his dream stayed tucked away in his dream drawer.

Before discussing why people don't take their dreams out of their drawers, let's understand why they put them there in the first place. Using your drawer as a convenient temporary storage place for dreams, while you're doing something else, is fine, but too many dreams stay stuffed away, never to become reality. This book will show you how to make your dream a reality.

Point of Information

The Business Plan: Blueprint for Black Ink

The business plan for your dream company needn't be complicated nor does it need to look professional. In fact, you can get waylaid by worrying too much about how it looks rather than what it says. These days, business plan forms are offered on software programs. Some budding entrepreneurs try to fit all their information into a plan using the form as a starting point. All too often, these entrepreneurs get bogged down—the software form becomes a strait jacket. They'd be better off writing their business plans on the back of an envelope.

Don't even try to formalize your plan at first. Instead, meet with your business friends and mentors. Describe your dream. Tell them about the resources you'll need and how you plan to use them; what you are going to do to pull it off. You should talk about the competition and how you expect to beat your rivals—or how you are going to make inroads in their market. When all this is talked through—when you have reasoned it out and feel it is exactly the way you want it to be—then you will be ready to do a precise business plan, with or without a form.

Meantime, your plan may be a page of scribbled notes with arrows pointing here and there. No one is grading format or penmanship. This is private stuff. You can even run your business with an informal plan. Do be thorough, however informal, and refine your plan as you go. And once you go to raise money, have a professional assist with the plan—to dot the i's and cross the t's.

Everyone Has a Dream Drawer

Would-be entrepreneurs aren't the only ones to have dream drawers. Many successful entrepreneurs have told me that they file their dreams. Some keep hundreds of ideas stored away; yet, they are still entrepreneurs.

Bill Veeck, former owner of the Chicago White Sox, once told me that he maintained a card file, with hundreds of index cards, each one containing a dream. He showed me one, an idea for a new type of hot dog with the mustard inside—a solution to millions of stained shirts. Despite having this dream and hundreds of others in his card file, he did pursue other dreams, and he was a successful and innovative entrepreneur. What was the difference between Bill Veeck and Milt Herzog, whose Zoggy Ball plan remained in the drawer?

Entrepreneurs like Bill Veeck have an open drawer policy. Either they have reached in the drawer and pulled out one or more dreams, in which case they are clearly entrepreneurs, or they intend to do so but are waiting for the right time. It doesn't matter how many dreams are in your drawer; what matters is whether you remove one. Taking that action requires a sensitivity to opportunity that lets you see your dream and a confidence in your ability to make your dream real. With that combination, you will feel compelled to take your dream out of the drawer. Before you know it, you can learn to be like Bill Veeck.

Point of Information

The Evolution of an Entrepreneurial Idea

As an entrepreneur, you must be focused, even though your focus may change over time. Your dream probably will turn out to be somewhat different in execution than in conception. Howard Ruff was right when he told me, "Most successful businesses start out with one idea and end up making their money on another. I started with one concept several times, and it's ended up in another direction, either as market conditions change or opportunities open up." That too is part of being a successful entrepreneur. Do not close your mind. You must be aware of changing circumstances that thwart your plans and react flexibly.

Capitalizing on Coincidence

Ed Beauvais had a dream that an airline company that operated efficiently, motivated its employees, and served its customers economically would succeed and rise above its fat, slow, lazy, and smug competition. Beauvais could not create deregulation, which would be vital, if his dream were to work. Then, coincidentally, the Reagan administration stepped in and established an era of deregulation in the airline industry. So Ed seized the opportunity provided by deregulation, and America West Airlines was born. A meaningful competitive factor, deregulation provided the environment that enabled Ed's entrepreneurship to take hold. The Gulf War, the recession, and Ed's inability to manage through those occurrences subsequently combined to create a different coincidence: Ed's departure and the company's seeking bankruptcy protection for a reorganization.

Sometimes, the coincidence is more subtle than a change of law, and, often, there is a series of coincidences. For centuries, fresh-baked goods could be bought in retail bakeries. But multiple locations of retail bakeries weren't economical. So, someone dreamed of packaging cookies and cakes, and that dream coincided with the packaging technology that allowed extended shelf life. Later, Charlie Lubin dreamed of ways of freezing, packaging, distributing, and marketing his baked goods. The quick-freezing technique made this possible. Lubin used it to create his dream, Sara Lee.

Point of Information

I Got a Million of 'Em

When the audience applauded comedian Jimmy Durante's lines, he'd pause and assure his audience: "I got a million of 'em."
The last thing you want to do when you attempt to sell financiers

on your idea is to boast about all your other ideas. That's like the fellow who tells a new girlfriend about all the other girls he's been dating. She'll lose interest, figuring she's just another port of call.

No matter how creative you were in devising your business concept, the concept is what interests potential investors. Your creativity is history to your backers; they don't care how creative you can be. They care how creative you were when you dreamed of the business they are buying into. That is the issue at hand, and if you can't focus on that, they'll figure you don't know how to manage. Your backers will want you to run things until the business gets big enough that they can afford to bring in a professional manager. That's assuming, of course, that you don't continue to manage the business yourself.

Talk about the business idea you brought to the financiers—the one that's going to make money for them. Don't get sidetracked. Bringing up other ideas is a common failing of entrepreneurs. Do it and you may not get the support you seek.

What Keeps Dreams in Drawers?

Excuses, myths, fear of failure, and better alternatives can cause you to keep your dreams tucked away and can become the basic barriers to your entrepreneurship. If you succumb to any of these, you may never be an entrepreneur. However, if you realize that there are only four—not hundreds or thousands—barriers to overcome, the path to becoming an entrepreneur seems easier.

Point of Information

I've Got a Secret

The dream drawer is a safe place to keep secrets. Every time you remove a secret and share it, you risk losing it. So, now, you have two reasons to leave additional ideas in the drawer, as well as two reasons to run quickly with your best idea.

If you don't believe you are at risk when you disclose business

secrets, ask humorist Art Buchwald. He showed an idea to
Paramount and, years later, Eddie Murphy turned up on
the silver screen in "Coming to America." Fortunately, Buchwald
was smart enough to register his idea with the Writer's Guild.
The movie was a mega-hit. Buchwald sued and won.

If an otherwise respectable giant, such as Paramount, will filch
an idea, you can't afford to take a chance that your secret is safe
with anybody. When it comes to business secrets, paranoia is not
an unhealthy frame of mind. As one of my partners often says,
even paranoids can have real enemies.

However, you'll need to reveal some information in order to
attract capital, employees, suppliers, and customers. For openers,
take a page from the U.S. Navy. Operate on a need-to-know
basis. Rarely does anyone need to know your whole story.
A customer will need to know that your product works.
A supplier will need to know the extent of customer demand
before he or she will extend credit. People you hope to hire may
be willing to sign up without details if you first send them to
satisfied customers.

If you have a great idea which cannot be protected by patent
and you're afraid to show it to a company that could make it
valuable because they might steal it, then you might want
to consider an about-to-disclose contract. You agree to disclose
a secret to someone and allow that person a short period to prove
that she or he already had the same idea. It is rarely possible to
create documentation on short notice of developing a novel idea.
If someone can prove prior knowledge, then he or she owes
you no obligation. But with no such prior coincident thought, the
person will be bound by the agreement.

Your secret should be viewed behind a glass, darkly. Use
intermediaries to validate your secret to customers, suppliers,
and others, without disclosing its nature. Consider hiring a
specialist in the field who will sign a contract barring disclosure.
Then, acting as a consultant, the specialist can confirm to those
you introduce that your secret is viable and do so without
revealing the nature of the secret itself.

Be sure to treat your secret as just that, a secret. Label the
relevant documents "confidential" and keep them locked up—
just as you would any other valuable.

Make your employees sign nondisclosure agreements, too. Explain that you trust them but that you have obligations to your investors, bankers, suppliers, customers, and other employees to safeguard your business opportunities. Tell each reluctant employee that you can't ask other workers to sign nondisclosures if he or she refuses to do so. That would imply you trust them less than you do him or her.

Thomas Edison was so proud of his work, he sometimes showed competitors how he did things. All too frequently, they would then steal his ideas. There's an old saying, a patent is a license to sue. Edison's patents were also must reading for rivals who then looked for ways around them. You should keep in mind that, whenever you patent something or secure a trademark or a copyright, you are revealing your secret— disclosing it to the entire world. Registration exclusivity and protection is the quid pro quo for moving that knowledge into the public domain. Before registration, be sure to treat your confidential ideas like the secrets they are.

The rules are quite different when it comes to investors. The securities laws require full disclosure of all material facts to potential investors. But nothing prevents you from obtaining a nondisclosure agreement from your investors. That's what I advise my clients in appropriate circumstances, and that's what Mary Anne Jackson of My Own Meals did, "Everyone I talked with signed one, or I didn't talk with them. In fact, only one person refused to sign."

Here is a caution regarding your boss's trade secrets: Some people start new businesses while they are still employed. If you are going to do that, you may need professional advice. You must be careful not to breach your employment agreement or your fiduciary obligations to your employer or *wrongfully make use of his or her trade secrets.* You can't afford to risk everything and then discover that your boss not only continues to own you but your new business as well.

4

Excuses You Use Not to Be an Entrepreneur

No epilogue I pray you, for your play needs no
excuse. Never excuse.
WILLIAM SHAKESPEARE
A Midsummer Night's Dream

There is an old saying, "We are all manufacturers. Some make good, others make trouble, and still others make excuses." Well, what do you want to manufacture? People never rave about how creative their excuses were. If you asked them, they wouldn't be proud of their excuses nor of subscribing to them. They probably would be shocked to realize they had used excuses, but by then, it's too late. It's not too late for you. There is no need for you to wake up later and realize you used excuses not to be an entrepreneur.

Garden Variety Excuses

By and large, the garden variety of excuses all fall into just a few categories. There is no limit to the ways people can express them; here are just a few examples of each.

The first category of excuses is "too much to lose":

"I can't risk my present position or my likely promotion."

"I can't afford to go without a salary."

"My kids are still in school."

"My spouse isn't working or doesn't make enough money to support us."

"I can't endanger the house or the nest egg."

The second category is lack of capital:

"It takes too much to start up."

"I don't know where to get enough money."

The third category of excuses reflects personal inadequacy:

"I'm too old, or too young, or too inexperienced."

"I can't handle that big a commitment of time."

"What if no one buys it?"

"Almost all new businesses fail."

The final category covers the competition or potential competition:

"How can I beat the big boys?"

"What if someone builds a better mousetrap?"

Do any of those excuses sound familiar? You may use different words but your own excuses probably aren't much different. If you buy any of them, you won't realize your dreams. Therefore, it is important for you to remember the excuses you have used and remove them.

Make a list of your own excuses. See if you can fit them into our four categories. If not, create more categories. Feel free to add to the list, from time to time, as you make more excuses. We will refer to your list later.

Sometimes, the apparent excuse hides the real one. Terri Bentz, a client of mine, started her business at home but had to make the plunge, sell her home, and open a real store if she were to grow it. She hesitated because she was too far in debt. She was spending more than she earned, and, if she sold her home, the recessed real estate market would result in a sale price lower than her investment. But her excuses, although true, were not the real reason. She remained at home because her home was her security blanket—it housed her business dream. She needed very little money to move the business to a store, but she didn't have it because her home was too expensive. I was able to help arrange capital for her once she agreed to sell her home. Terri moved to a rental apartment which reduced her debt and monthly expenses and left her free to concentrate on growing her business.

Millions of people could have used the same excuses as you but instead have opted for entrepreneurial success. Those people were no more able than you, but their dreams were more important than their excuses. You can develop that attitude— that your dream is more important to you than your excuses. To start, you must understand your excuses and why you use them. Now that we've discussed the garden variety excuses, what about the extraordinary excuses?

Conventional Wisdoms

Some excuses are so commonly believed that they rise to the level of conventional wisdoms. Just 20 years ago, it was generally accepted that only the U.S. Post Office could deliver mail in this country. Many people believed that federal laws prohibited others from doing it. As the conventional wisdom, the belief provided a reasonable excuse for not exploring a private mail delivery enterprise, even though everyone knew that the Post Office was doing a terrible job. Then, in the early 1970s, Fred Smith rejected this conventional wisdom and founded Federal Express.

Fred first wrote about his plan to compete with the Post Office while an undergraduate at Yale. His economics professor at Yale read about the idea in a paper Fred turned in for credit. The professor gave him a C and told him that the idea wouldn't fly. Even so, Fred believed in the dream and in his ability to pull it off.

Shortly after Smith formed Federal Express, the Arab oil embargo dramatically increased fuel costs, making his projections obsolete and jeopardizing his company's future. All the experts told him that because the wings of his dream were coated with oil, it would never fly and he should postpone his takeoff. Everyone "knew" that a private mail carrier could not survive the increased fuel costs. Smith could have used the experts' reactions as an excuse; instead, once again, he ignored them.

[Incidentally, Fred Smith told me that his greatest childhood interest was reading about great leaders in history. He spent much of his childhood reading about Hannibal and his elephant trek to carry his message (and army) across the Alps. With that background, I'm surprised that Federal Express's logo wasn't Dumbo.]

Edwin Masters* was a machine tool operator who became an entrepreneur. He immigrated to the United States with a good background in machinery and machine tools but with neither a good education nor experience at running a business. At one of his first jobs in the United States, he saw a way to improve a production technique and thought about turning his new-found secret into a business. There were plenty of garden variety excuses to stop Edwin. He had no capital, needed a steady job to support his family, and spoke English with a foreign accent.

Even more intimidating were the accepted wisdoms. Edwin's production secret was not patentable, and his only potential customer was a *Fortune* 500 company, which would not look favorably upon a poorly capitalized source of supply for an important component. Conventional wisdom—and everyone Edwin spoke with—said it was a "no-go." He was advised to attempt to sell the secret to the giant corporation and take a small royalty but not to gamble everything on a start-up business which lacked protection or stature. Edwin, however, wasn't buying the excuses; he was too busy buying his dream.

Edwin started his business and, before long, became so critical to his *Fortune* 500 customer's business that the firm offered to build, at its expense, a back-up plant, in case his plant burned down. Fewer than 10 years after he began, he sold his business—actually his secret—for millions, all because Edwin rejected the excuses, including those accepted wisdoms.

Profile

Edwin Masters and the Midnight Tweak

It is hard to believe that anyone could sell "fine tuning" to a *Fortune* 500 company for millions of dollars. But that is precisely what Edwin Masters did. His secret process constituted the way that he adjusted his machinery.

His problem was keeping this fact secret from his many employees. For a determined entrepreneur, the solution was straightforward and simple. Each morning, Masters turned up at 5:30 a.m.—before anyone else arrived. He would adjust the internal mechanism and then lock up the machine. That was only half of the job. Masters had to put in a long day, for Masters couldn't leave until the last production line employee punched out. At that point, he would unlock the machinery, undo the adjustment, clean the machine, and go home. This eliminated the risk that workers who came to clean and lubricate the equipment would learn his secret.

It would have been easy for Fred Smith to believe that only the Post Office could deliver the mail or that the oil embargo made a fuel-sensitive business inadvisable.

Edwin Masters could have succumbed to the warnings against basing a business on an unpatentable secret and being a poorly capitalized source of supply for a giant corporation. Both would have been justified in following the conventional wisdom and using it as an excuse. But entrepreneurs refuse to let their fears hold them back.

5

Myths That Stop You

We are handicapped by policies based on old
myths rather than current realities.
JAMES WILLIAM FULBRIGHT

Myths can interfere with entrepreneurial vision. If you think getting into a boat is difficult, imagine how hard it would be if you believed there were dragons waiting in the water. That's what myths do. They create dragons.

I want you to stop believing in those myths. But stopping someone from believing in something is difficult to do. I have always advised against arguing with a person's beliefs when you can argue with their knowledge, for most people believe far more than they know. Therefore, I will expose some common beliefs—these myths—so you know what the facts are and see how the myths distort the reality. Then, you can easily challenge and overcome the myths.

The Chauvinist Myth

One myth is that men are better able to be entrepreneurs than women. This myth is not promulgated exclusively by male chauvinists; it is also spread by some highly credentialed people. For example, Professor Van Harlow of the University of Arizona found an inverse relationship between the body's enzyme levels and risk aversion. Men's naturally lower enzyme levels, he concluded, make them more willing to take risks than women, and, therefore, better entrepreneurial candidates.

Dr. Harlow's research sounds convincing but was not based on a valid scientific study and didn't prove his premise. Actually, no conclusive studies show that men are born entrepreneurs and women aren't. My women clients and my interviewees for this book attest to that. So does the fact that, currently, two-thirds of all new businesses are begun by women.

Although I also can't claim scientific validity, my survey did reveal some differences between male and female entrepreneurs. For example, when I asked entrepreneurs why they wanted to be entrepreneurs, men used the word *control*, whereas women used the word *independence*. Actually, women and men are probably using different words for the same concept. The use of the different words has nothing to do with biological differences. The different words reflect societal stereotypes, such as male dominance. The goal of many men is to dominate (control), whereas women who view the world as male-dominated seek independence from that dominance. Holly Hunt, who founded the largest showroom in Chicago's Merchandise Mart, used both words, but she referred to controlling herself, not others. Controlling yourself is very much like being independent, and that is what matters to entrepreneurs. After all, it's your destiny you want to control.

Different Genders, Different Dreams

There is nothing inherent in gender that requires men and women to have different entrepreneurial dreams. In our society, boys and girls have been raised with different interests and pursuits. Those differences in upbringing often result in different dreams, different approaches, and different timing in pursuing the dreams. Women and men dream different dreams because they have lived different lives and their dreams emerge from their environment and training in the past. Women who were raised to be homemakers, for instance, tend to develop businesses, products, or services that deal with the home, because that is their expertise.

When Sybil Ferguson, the founder of Diet Center, first thought of helping people lose weight, she did it as a favor for her doctor's patients. Debbi Fields served cookies to her husband's clients in her home before founding Mrs. Fields Cookies. Evelyn Echols' school trains the travel industry's employees. Her first class was for juvenile delinquents, an idea that came from a conversation during a business dinner she attended with her husband. Eileen Ford, confined to her home as a new mother, agreed to take phone messages for a few friends who were models, and thus started the Ford Model Agency. Sheila Cluff, who founded Sheila's Spas, the owner of The Palms at Palm Springs and The Oaks at Ojai, learned the value and techniques of upgrading physical fitness training while a physical education teacher. She saw her peers seeking help in becoming physically fit and began by helping them, on the side.

Point of Information

Banking on Femininity

If there were records of the number of would-be women entrepreneurs who are turned down by the banks, the percentage would no doubt be a great deal higher than for men. Even so, the reason for the turn-down is not always gender-based. Sherren Leigh, the savvy and well-connected entrepreneur and publisher of the pioneering newspaper *Today's Chicago Woman,* says the problems women have relate to the types of businesses they run and to inexperience in business matters.

The other problem is cultural. Until the 1960s and 1970s, many women were homemakers and were either confined to or contented in this role. So, as society changed and women began moving into the world, they lacked the skills their husbands acquired in business. Even after women entered the business world and opened their own businesses, things were different for them. Most women set up service businesses. Banks want collateral for their loans. There is little inventory in a service business, so there is no collateral for the bank.

When women start a new business, they tend to bring suitable talent to the table at least as often as men do. However, the playing field is not always level. Women still have a greater burden in convincing bankers and investors. Often, women don't have the background simply to write that all-important document, the business plan. Where a man can get away without a formal business plan, if a woman goes in without one, she will not get the money she seeks.

If you don't have the background to prepare a formal business plan, don't give up. Many men and women have graduated from business schools these days who are available as consultants to people like you. Or if you have a friend who did so, you probably should consider asking his or her help. Otherwise network with such people or with people who know them. Do so by all means.

It may not be fair that women need formal business plans even more than men, but you must decide whether you want to make a business of a cause or cause a business. Your business plan is your passkey to a passbook filled with the bank's money.

All those women first applied their dreams to avocations. They tested their dreams in the nonentrepreneurial settings where they were comfortable. The entrepreneurial side of their dreams arose later. Milton Herzog, however, did not try using Zoggy Ball in his district's schools, although, as superintendent, he could have used that forum to test the product. Instead, he saved Zoggy Ball for the ultimate entrepreneurial application, which he ultimately never pursued. His dream remained a dream.

The point is that gender is not an impediment but an opportunity. By recognizing your background and appreciating the experiences and influences it provided, you will know where your dream is likely to come from and that where you come from enables you to convert your dream to reality.

Women May Weigh Less But Aren't Lightweights

Mary Kay Ash, the founder of Mary Kay Cosmetics, identified another factor dissuading women from becoming entrepreneurs. She became an entrepreneur despite the fact that, or perhaps because, women were never taken seriously. It's bad enough that not being taken seriously increases the difficulty of starting and building a business—getting investors, bankers, suppliers, customers, employees, and advisors. But, when it causes you to question your own dream or lack the confidence that you can get the job done, then not being taken seriously decreases your prospects of becoming an entrepreneur, and the myth becomes reality.

Mary Kay also told me an interesting story about how she got started that demonstrates how a potential myth—location, location, location are the three most important factors in a retail business—can be relegated to a minor annoyance. She referred to the myth as a roadblock; her entrepreneurship enabled her to take a detour.

Mary Kay's first store was located on the main floor of an office building. She understood the critical importance of location and selected the site because of the heavy traffic of office workers. However, on the first day, Mary Kay saw a problem. She had considered the location but, due to her lack of experience, had failed to realize that the office workers would pass by only while rushing to and from work, or on a quick coffee break, without time for a cosmetics treatment and lesson. She could have closed the business, blaming it on a lack of experience or understanding. Instead, she found a way around the roadblock, by learning to give 15-minute facials.

Point of Information

Scouting for Location

Location is the paramount consideration in real estate. Even so, the best location for one business is not necessarily the best location for another. Obvious though this may be, many a business leases inappropriate space at outrageous cost.

We know that as apartment renters it makes sense to hold rents at 25 percent of take-home pay. There is no rule of thumb for entrepreneurs on rent. A fast food business grossing $250,000 a year would consider a $2000 a month rent a steal. But a fabric store grossing $50,000 and paying similar rent in the same space is doomed.

Different types of businesses—retail, manufacturing, distribution, and office—have different location needs. A retailer dreams of a higher traffic area, such as in a shopping mall. A computer assembly plant needs a location that is accessible by car—even if it is in the boondocks. A manufacturer of ranges may chose a location mainly because it is on a rail siding.

Heavy traffic is a dream or a nightmare depending upon whether you are a retailer or a company with an office building next to a rush hour bottleneck. Even a retailer on a busy road must be certain passersby can slip off the road and ease to a stop. Also, keep parking restrictions in mind.

Zoning and lease covenants that affect operations affect tenants differently. Mall leases often require tenants to remain open for extended hours, increasing payroll costs. That clause, unnoticed, can send the unwitting retailer's "rent" costs to prohibitive levels.

Certain locations entitle you to government assistance with financing, favorable tax treatment, or both, but these incentives must be balanced against other considerations. Sheila Cluff, the fitness instructor, might have received important government aid had she opened her spa in the depressed Appalachia areas of Pennsylvania or West Virginia. But she guessed that fitness would become important in California first. Customer potential was far more important than government assistance, so she moved her family to the Golden State and lived richly ever after.

Nobody banks in a tumble-down shack. But if your business doesn't need a posh setting for credibility, don't waste valuable resources on real estate or rent. Jack Miller kept start-up costs low by starting Quill Corporation in his father-in-law's garage. Quill now has facilities befitting 9- or 10-digit businesses that provide the image and efficiency which make the business more productive and foster further growth.

Dealing with the myth that women aren't as likely to be entrepreneurs, or as good as male entrepreneurs, may be a short-term problem. Societal stereotypes are changing, and more women are choosing to be entrepreneurs. Women need no longer be relegated to what Gloria Steinem labels "pink collar workers." Women can become their own bosses and wear whatever color collars they want. In fact, they are. Of the hundreds of thousands of new businesses formed in each of the last few years, about two-thirds of them were formed by women. I wonder how these statistics figure into Dr. Harlow's "mythical" equation.

The point is that men are no more capable than women of being entrepreneurs. People in general are better prepared in areas where they have had greater opportunities for experience. Entrepreneurship is an equal opportunity and guarantees that you will be the same gender as your boss.

A good example of the new breed of woman entrepreneur is Leslie Hindman.

Profile

Leslie Hindman and an Antique Prejudice

When Leslie Hindman decided to fire her boss and hire herself, she went to her father for money to finance her plan for an antique business. Don Hindman was a Chicago entrepreneur who had worked hard for many years before selling out to Irish tycoon Michael Smurfit.

When Leslie approached Don Hindman for a loan, he snapped at her: "You're out of your cotton-pickin' mind. You get married and have babies like you're supposed to!" With that, she stormed out of the house. Her confidence was shaken—not to mention her dignity as a human being. She sought out friends for bruised-ego repair. The late real estate magnate Arthur Rubloff was one mentor.

Then she took a page from her father's book. Don Hindman argues that managed companies grow by momentum. He insists entrepreneurs don't have that advantage. They have to make things happen. Leslie set off to do just that. She petitioned other potential backers with all the fervor of a young Don Hindman.

Shortly thereafter, Don Hindman got an evening phone call. He remembers Leslie said, "Dad, you missed a good deal. I got my $100,000 today." Don asked, "Who from?" Leslie said, "My backers, and you're not one of them," and hung up.

Leslie's antique auction firm, which bears her name, grew to become the largest in the Midwest and has put some great old things on the block. She won international recognition when her firm discovered an original Van Gogh in a Wisconsin home. Most important, she proved that injecting gender into entrepreneurship is an antique notion.

Immigration: A Gateway to Entrepreneurship

Some myths are based on facts but are still myths and are deceptive anyway. Ever notice how many immigrants are entrepreneurs? A high percentage of immigrants do become entrepreneurs. That's a fact, but there are many false conclusions as to why so many become entrepreneurs. Many immigrants start businesses because they can't get jobs due to language and culture differences, or bias and bigotry. And the numbers are increasing. The number of small businesses in the United States owned by Asian and Pacific Islander Americans increased 87 percent between 1982 and 1987 (compared to the 13 percent national average, according to Lynn Choy Uyeda, president of the Asian American Advertising and P.R. Alliance of Los Angeles). A large part of that 87 percent increase represents businesses run by newcomers to the United States.

All people who want to be entrepreneurs, immigrants or not, are attracted to the control or independence their own business would offer. Many people, however, attribute "foreigners" with special, inborn, entrepreneurial talents. That is one myth; here's another: some believe the secret lies in why they came here. Actually, many came because they had heard the streets were paved with gold, and they dreamed of picking up their share.

As a lad in Hungary, Otto Clark worked for and admired his

aunt, an entrepreneur who ran a grocery/silo business. When the Russians invaded, Otto came to the United States, where he worked briefly for a large company. Five years after arriving here, he started his first company which went public and ultimately was sold. In 1977, he founded Clark Copy Company, his third company, which became the first U.S. company to sell to Communist China—a true irony in light of his prior flight from Hungary's communism and repression. Although he had worked for other U.S. companies, Otto, perhaps remembering why he admired his aunt, perhaps for many other reasons, wanted his own business.

Kim Soon Ro is a barber. Born and raised in Korea, she had been happy there, until her parents committed her to an arranged marriage. When her husband decided to emigrate to the United States, she followed dutifully, hoping for independence. (She achieved some independence when she divorced her husband.) For a while, she worked for a barbershop, developing skills and improving her English. Eventually, she opened her own shop. Coming from overseas, that was inevitable—right?

These stories present two very different people from very different parts of the world but both wanted to be entrepreneurs to control their own destinies. Although Otto and Kim may *want* to be and have to be entrepreneurs for the same reasons as some of those born here, what enables them to become entrepreneurs is quite different. They have already seen a precious dream, that of a new homeland, and they have already done what it took to make it real—they emigrated. Now, they are attuned to that process, and, when they see their entrepreneurial dream, they are prepared to go for it. In fact, for them, it may seem easy, compared with their earlier act of going for it.

Ethnic Minorities

Racial myths are destructive for social reasons we all understand. Myths also can dissuade those who misunderstand the negative implications and falsely comfort those who misapply the positive implications.

African Americans constitute 12 percent of the U.S. population and own between 2 percent and 3 percent of the U.S. businesses. They have been slower to take advantage of America's entrepreneurial opportunities, leading some—whites and blacks—to subscribe to a myth that African Americans are less capable of doing so. That is a destructive myth, since it often becomes a self-fulfilling prophecy.

Steps are being taken, by government, business, and individuals, to improve the situation. Mentors are creating role models who create entrepreneurs, and each step has geometric proportions. Laws, customs, and experience, as well as pressure and reinvestment by blacks, are easing and eliminating barriers. In time, the situation will improve. However, the critical point is that there are identifiable reasons for the statistics, and the myths are false.

A good friend, a banker, who heard I was interviewing hundreds of entrepreneurs for this book, asked me if I found that most entrepreneurs are Jewish. Actually, Jews constitute a small minority of U.S. entrepreneurs, although perhaps a somewhat larger percentage than population demographics would indicate. My friend was well-meaning and curious. Others, however, have turned such myths into the basis for bigotry. And some might believe their ethnic background qualifies them, when they are not truly qualified. Perhaps there's a banker who believes the myth and makes loans he shouldn't make.

Profile

George Johnson: Casting for a Role Model

It's a lot harder to lift yourself by your bootstraps when you have no boots. During the Depression, George Johnson's family was so poor his mother laid it on the line by making it very clear that "she could not afford to even keep us in the apartment we were in on the salary she made, $11 a week." George found ways to make money "because I had to."

At age six, George went up and down the back stairs in the 24-apartment building they lived in. He always arrived before the janitor. He went through every garbage can in the back halls on every floor. George pulled out the milk bottles and the newspapers. Then he took them to the junk man in the alley who weighed the papers, counted the bottles, and handed over the pennies that George had earned.

George wasn't too proud to follow another trade that some like to stigmatize. When he was nine, his aunt paid the janitor in George's building to make him a shoeshine box. His aunt then gave George the money he needed to buy supplies.

"I used to walk from 34th Street in Chicago down to the 12th Street train station every Saturday morning, stopping on the way at the police station....This was a motor pool, and there were motorcycles. The cycle police wore leggings and high-topped shoes. I used to shine those shoes for a nickel." Then he went to the middle of the block between 11th and 12th Streets and shined shoes of people going to and from the train station. So George made a buck in 1936—the depths of the Depression.

George's aunt remained a cheerleader. She taught him about the finer things: theater, classical music, and riding, which became George's passion. When George could afford it, he bought himself boots and a riding habit and wore them through the neighborhood "looking like a freak." He was determined to stand out. George was an entrepreneur by nature: "I acted different because I thought I was different."

Obviously, George was a self-starter, but he needed a role model, someone who could mentor him. Mentors for young black men were very scarce back then. Not just any mentor would do. Johnson says blacks aren't challenged by whites: "We know whites have a different kind of background. The challenge comes from blacks, because we know that a black man comes from similar circumstances." After graduating from high school, George was lucky to find work with S. B. Fuller, whom George calls the "most dynamic black businessman of his time." Fuller began his cosmetics business with $25, in 1936, the year George began shining shoes. By 1945, when George went to work for him, S. B. Fuller was doing in excess of $300,000 a year. In the years that George worked for him, S. B. Fuller grew the business to about $5 million. Fuller, says Johnson, was "like an evangelist...his whole philosophy was based on the Christian

principle. His mission was to teach people to assume the
responsibility for themselves and to make their own living. He
went out and got people who were unemployed and showed
them how to make more money than they had ever made
by selling door to door. I was exposed to this. I saw this man
achieve what he achieved." George goes on to add: "We believe
we can do what we see other black people doing. If he can do it, I
can do it. As a result of that, I have found a lot of competition
for my company, Johnson Products, because guys look at
me, saying 'George Johnson is not any smarter than I am. I can do
what he is doing and make it in the business.' And they do it."

George Johnson's company, which makes cosmetics for African
Americans, was the first black-owned business to go public. That
made George Johnson a role model to African-American
entrepreneur wannabes. The lesson for all wannabes is to find a
role model that fits, one whose example can teach you and
challenge you. Having a role model of similar background—
ethnic, gender, socio-economic—is important for some.

George Johnson's Secret Weapon: That Little White Lie

George Johnson, like so many other entrepreneurs, was willing
to bend the truth when he could do it without hurting anybody.
He was forced to do just that to launch Johnson Products. The
year was 1954, and George needed $250. At the loan company,
he fell into the trap that lies waiting for many entrepreneurs. If
starting your business entails a full-time commitment, you must
quit your existing job, and you will, in the view of many
bankers, become unemployed. Banks rarely lend to the unemployed.

So George followed a simple expedient. He went to another
office of the same company and said he wanted money to take
his wife on a vacation. He said he would repay the money with
continuing paychecks from his "existing" job. He got the loan,
quit his job, and used the "vacation money" to start Johnson
Products.

Entrepreneurs Are
Super Heroes

Another myth is that an entrepreneur is a super hero, who leaps tall challenges in a single bound. More people than are willing to admit believe the super heroes myth and use it as a rationale for not pursuing their dream. After all, if entrepreneurs are super heroes, then why bother to compete? Until you overcome this myth and stop believing it, you can't become an entrepreneur.

Judd Malkin and Neil Bluhm were cofounders of JMB Realty, which today controls over $20 billion of property and which *Business Week* described as having "a Midas touch in a mushy market." Judd and Neil had been friends for years. Judd knew Neil was very smart. Neil had won the gold medal on the CPA exam and was the rising star at his old-line, prestigious law firm. The problem was that Judd thought everyone in the business world was like Neil. He told me that only when he learned otherwise —when he overcame the myth that everyone was a super hero like Neil—was he able to start a business. Of course, he took out a little insurance by starting JMB with Neil.

Barry Potekin, founder of Gold Coast Dogs and an *Inc. Magazine* "Entrepreneur of the Year," believed that businesspeople possessed mystical powers. When Barry was a kid, he watched his father play cards with his cronies, all of whom were businesspeople. To Barry, they all seemed to speak in a mystical language about mystical things. He viewed them and all businesspeople as part of a Cabal, a group of mystics not unlike the super hero Cabalistic mystics of Jewish lore.

It wasn't until Barry stopped buying the myth—until he realized that businesspeople were not part of a Cabal—that Barry could start his own business. Only when he was able to see them as they really were—merely good businesspeople—could he become an entrepreneur.

Children of the Pioneers

Barry, in fact, had something of a head start. He came from entrepreneurial stock. However, it is by no means necessary that you have this background. In the course of my discussions with entrepreneurs, I have found nothing to sustain the myth that entrepreneurs are children of entrepreneurs. A great many entrepreneurs come from families where entrepreneurship was neither practiced nor understood. Many emigrants from the Soviet Union to free-market countries have taken easily and quickly to entrepreneurship. Most of their parents and leaders were communists, so they had to look beyond their parents and Karl Marx for role models. As Israeli entrepreneur Stef Wertheimer says of recent Soviet emigres, "Instead of learning from Marx and Engels, they must start concentrating on Marks and Spencer."

The Debtor's Prison Myth

Some Americans are a bit foggy on the well-established fact that there is no debtor's prison in this country. So long as you are honest in the way you borrow, you don't have to worry about arrest. You will not go to jail if you go broke owing money to suppliers, employees, and everyone else. Honesty in borrowing means not lying and fully disclosing the facts the lender needs to know to rationally decide whether to loan you money. The loan application must include all liabilities, including contingent liabilities, such as your guarantee of your brother-in-law's bank loan.

Of course, nothing requires you to include all your assets on the application. Lenders aren't hurt if they agree to loans to applicants who are more affluent than they appear. Then, the omitted assets may not be part of the lender's requested collateral. Also, in certain circumstances, if estate planning procedures involve transfers to family members, some assets may be safeguarded from creditors.

Profile

Jim Covert: Life after Bankruptcy

Jim Covert was the youngest in a family of four children, but he was easily the most ambitious. He was only a boy when he set up his first business in Danville, Illinois.

Jim's dad, Colonel Covert, who started as an Army private at 17, became a highly decorated soldier in the European theater. Later, in the Pacific, he survived the infamous Bataan death march in World War II. The family's problems began when he retired.

Command officers and their families live well in the armed services. Though poorly paid by civilian standards, colonels are subsidized and catered to. They are assigned upper-middle-class housing. The low prices at the Post Exchange stretch salaries, and there are generous food allowances. Colonels have chauffeurs and other valuable perks.

Back in Danville, Illinois, the Covert family was financially strapped. Eventually, Jim's father set up his own concrete construction business. Even though Jim was still in grade school, Jim just naturally pitched in to help. Jim says: "I used to spend my summers making precast concrete footsteps. Dad would go out and build patios out of these things. It was a horrible existence."

The business did poorly. His father was frustrated, and the family suffered. The Colonel's business finally went belly up. Jim was 14 at the time. This was painful but Jim learned a priceless lesson: "I found out at a very early age that there really is life after bankruptcy. It's not something to be really that much afraid of. We [had been living] miserably. But two weeks after he filed the papers in court…, Dad landed a very good job. The whole family started living much better.

"I think people have a real fear of going bankrupt. I got exposed to that when I was very young. It never scared me…, I was never afraid of failing. I never got embarrassed because something didn't work right. I figure you learn from it and you go on and do something else. You don't have to make the same mistakes again."

Jim was the youngest man ever to serve in the Secret Service, where he protected three Presidents, including Richard Nixon, who, for Jim, had been a true father figure.

Jim's secret service training and experience was helpful when he joined a security system installation and monitoring business called SecurityLink. But his early exposure to his father's bankruptcy and his later observation, from a close and unique perspective, of the tumultuous end of the Nixon presidency, helped Jim at SecurityLink. When he arrived at the company, the business was already in trouble, and Jim wound up replacing his boss and assuming the helm of two corporations, one of which already had filed for bankruptcy. SecurityLink is now the nation's tenth largest security company, and Jim is clearly its entrepreneur. Jim, a natural entrepreneur, was energized by his father's and President Nixon's failures, not defeated by them.

Bust the Myths That Could Stop You

Kids believe in two types of myths: those based on fantasies and intended to cause fun, such as Santa Claus and the Tooth Fairy, and those that sound factual and are intended to convince you to do what is good for you, such as eat everything on your plate "because there are people starving in Europe." I wanted to help the people starving in Europe and never questioned how my eating would affect those starving people. Now, I realize that some of those people who were starving in Europe can fit into the European clothes that don't fit me.

Fantasy-based myths are easy to dismiss. When older children told you there was no Santa Claus, a simple nod of agreement by your parents destroyed the myth. Busting myths that appear to be factual is not simple. The extra step required to realize that the myth is not factual is worthwhile because, if not busted, these myths gain increased credibility and become more difficult to destroy. So let's start now.

Stop

Myths are like the dividing lines on the freeway. They guide your drive, but you don't really notice them. When the road forks and the dividing lines bend both ways, you must stop, reorient yourself, and make a decision. The same is true of myths. You believe them, let them guide you, but you don't even notice they exist. To break myths, you must notice them. You must stop and see them for what they are. If you ignore them, their blurred images will continue as a ribbon of influence.

Separate

Myths don't just happen. They are repeated by people you trust, such as parents, teachers, role models, peers, and the media—at a time when you are susceptible to this influence. Now you must reject that influence and separate the myth from its source. So imagine that the myth is told to you by someone other than its influential source. Imagine that the last person you caught lying to you told you the myth. Now, what do you think of the information?

Scrutinize

Myths consist of two parts: the underlying apparent truths and the syllogism that leads to a conclusion. For example: *A equals B and B equals C* are assumptions that are apparent truths. *Therefore, A must equal C* is the analysis of those apparent truths.

It's easy to see how underlying assumptions can be false, and much more difficult to see how the analysis of the apparent truths can lead to a false conclusion. For example, consider Judd Malkin's myth that all businesspeople (entrepreneurs) are like Neil Bluhm. Judd, you will recall, hesitated to become an entrepreneur because he believed the following myth: *Neil Bluhm is extremely smart, and Neil Bluhm is a businessperson (entrepreneur).* Then the analysis of the apparent truths was: *Therefore, all businesspeople (entrepreneurs) are extremely smart, posing a competitive threat.*

Both assumptions are accurate, but the analysis fails because, although Bluhm is *an* entrepreneur, he is not *all* entrepreneurs. Recognizing the analytic flow requires scrutiny, blended with suitable doses of skepticism and cynicism. Only when Judd Malkin examined other businesspeople and discovered that they were not like Neil could he become an entrepreneur.

There are more myths. Knowing them all is not as important as realizing that they exist, identifying them when they surface, examining them rationally, and putting them to rest. Don't let myths impede your progress.

6
Fear of Failure

The only thing we have to fear is fear itself.
PRESIDENT FRANKLIN DELANO ROOSEVELT

People also leave their dreams unfulfilled because of their fear of failure. Fear of failure may sound like an excuse or a myth, but it is different. Excuses are worries about factors you don't know about or whose validity you don't check out. Myths are ideas you believe and accept as true, without knowing whether they are founded on truths or lies. Belief in myths is a form of naivete.

Fear of failure is different. Even after you investigate the facts painstakingly, learn the truths and reject the lies, fear of failure prevents you from becoming an entrepreneur, because you still lack the self-confidence to know you'll succeed. Terror leads to immobility.

When you stop using excuses and no longer believe in myths but are still afraid to follow your dream, then, as I've said to clients on many occasions, it's probably fear—a terror you have inside you—about whether your dream is valid or whether you have what it takes to get the job done. Ironically, that terror, that fear of failure, can become the vehicle to help you make the move. To master the fear of failure, you must first understand it.

Profile

Debbi Fields: This Cookie Doesn't Crumble Anymore

You would think that the best looking girl in her high school class—the head cheerleader and every male classmate's idea of a dream come true—would have confidence dripping from her fingertips. But Debbi Fields' parents inadvertently damaged her ego. Debbi was the youngest of five attractive and talented sisters. Her parents steadfastly refused to praise her—or any of her sisters—individually.

They said, "We are proud of you" but invariably added "like we are of all of your sisters. You are *all* special." Debbi actually rebelled to get attention. She became a tomboy and, in a stunning success for a young girl, she became the first female "batboy" for the Oakland A's baseball team. She also neglected her studies and didn't go to college. In fact, she learned so little at school that she regrets it to this day. The lack of support at home had a lasting impact. Despite her beauty and her fine athletic skills, Debbi suffered low self-esteem.

This insecurity persisted after her marriage. Husband Randy is a consultant—an innovative thinker with clients among the *Fortune* 500 companies. One day, while Randy was busy, Debbi was chatting with one of his clients at the Fields' home near Silicon Valley. She misused a word and the client corrected her. She was simultaneously mortified and motivated. When Randy returned, she fled to the kitchen and baked cookies. Her vocabulary might have been lacking, but it didn't affect her confidence that she could make great cookies.

What Debbi lacked in self-esteem, she made up for in ambition. She was determined not to let her feelings of inferiority stand in the way of success. One day, she told Randy that she wanted to open a cookie stand at the local mall. Randy—who can be blunt—told her flatly she would be an absolute failure but agreed to lend her the $50,000 she needed to equip a store with professional bakery equipment. Even so, Randy bet Debbi she wouldn't do $50 at retail on her first day in the busy shopping mall.

The night before she opened, Debbi lost all confidence. What if

Randy was right? Wasn't he, after all, clever enough that some of the nation's top business leaders came to him for advice? She cried all night before the opening. In her torment, she convinced herself that she could fail: "I thought about what it would be like for me. I would disappoint so many people. I felt really alone and really depressed."

The next day, the excitement was back. The realization that she could fail boosted her adrenalin. But reality sank in again shortly after she opened the store. Nobody walked into her little shop. She began to wonder if she would do any business at all. Finally, she had an inspiration. She grabbed a tray and piled it high with steaming cookies. She locked the door behind her and walked into the crowd, giving away the unsalable cookies as she made her way through the mall. Even though her cookies weren't selling, she had no sense of the humiliation that stymies wannabe entrepreneurs. (Wannabes are those who don't realize that false pride has no place in an entrepreneur's personality.) Instead, Debbi was filled with a sense of adventure, and her cookies sold like hot cakes. In no time, patrons were seeking out her store.

At first, it didn't occur to Debbi that her idea could be duplicated even once. But one store led to two, and two led to two hundred, and hundreds created a countrywide chain of Mrs. Fields Cookies stores. Mrs. Fields Cookies are now a national institution.

Long after her success with Mrs. Fields Cookies, she found out that her father did, in fact, think she was special. But it happened after he died. After the funeral, one of Debbi's sisters went through his personal effects, including his wallet. She showed Debbi the two pictures he carried around. One was of the whole family. The other one was of one of the girls. It was Debbi. She says that was the first time she realized that her father knew that she was different.

Even so, she still feels insecure from time to time—like everybody else. Every businessperson has setbacks. There was the time the business expanded too rapidly and nearly ran out of capital. But Debbi always puts her fears aside and focuses on success—self-improvement, too. "I am pleased when I see that I have done a job well. But I'm personally never satisfied [I never

accomplish] what I think I am capable of...." Debbi's favorite
saying is "Good enough never is."

Like most big winners, Debbi isn't satisfied. She still constantly
looks for new challenges and new successes—such as the ailing
bread store chain she took over and nursed back to health.
Recently, Mrs. Fields Cookies has had serious financial setbacks.
Debbi's equity position and compensation has been substantially
decreased, and Randy has left the company's employ. But Debbi
is a cookie that doesn't crumble. For Debbi, there will be more
challenges and more successes.

Debbi Fields' Secret Weapon

By the late 1960s, U.S. retailers were leaving the nation's central
cities and relocating in the malls. Shoppers spent hours under
the mall's roof and needed a snack to tide them over. That's
when the possibility of reaching a mass market with fresh-baked
cookies occurred to Debbi. Compact ovens had been developed
that would fit into small stores, making the idea practical from a
technical point of view. She bought the equipment, developed
her trademark recipe, and filled a previously unoccupied market niche.

Failing Ain't Bad

Eleanor Roosevelt said, "You gain strength, courage and confidence by every experience in which you really stop to look fear
in the face." Failing doesn't make you a failure. Do you consider
Babe Ruth, Ted Williams, Joe DiMaggio, and Willie Mays failures? Well, every one of them failed to get a hit over 60 percent
of their times at bat. Do you consider Michael Jordan, Wayne
Gretzky, and Herschel Walker failures? Jordan and Gretzky miss
many shots, and Walker almost always gets tackled short of the
goal line, yet they get paid millions each year to fail much of the
time. No one can deny that President Clinton was a successful
candidate, even though he failed to get the majority of the popular vote. You see, failing is part of life, but so is success.

Concentrate on succeeding, not on failing. Then, when you do fail, accept it as human behavior and convert it to a positive. Remember the story about the boy who entered a room filled up to his chin with manure. Instead of just seeing a room full of manure, he said that, somewhere in the room, there must be a pony! That's what I mean by converting a failure to a positive.

Over the years, I have represented a number of Indy Car drivers. They are a special breed of athlete, enduring ordeals that are both physically and emotionally vigorous. They have many entrepreneurial traits, but most prominent is that they are absolutely fearless of failure. In the movie *Days of Thunder*, Tom Cruise portrays a race car driver and says, "I'm more afraid of bein' nothin' than I am of bein' hurt." That is the spirit behind entrepreneurial success.

In the long run failing may be better for you. It is a lot like getting vaccinated, the pain is momentary but improves your life in the long run. Failure teaches you that failing isn't fatal. That's a lesson best learned first-hand. Failing teaches you what not to do and, thus, how to succeed. It also strengthens your resistance to barriers and your resolve to hurdle them. It develops character, and, if nothing else, entrepreneurs have character. I tell would-be entrepreneurs, "There are no losers, only winners and learners." Is that hard for you to believe? Then listen to some people whose failings made them wiser and more successful.

Ed Beauvais, the founder of America West Airlines, is an accountant by education and background. He told me he once interviewed for a job in the accounting department of an airline but was rejected because he had failed the CPA exam. That was a double whammy—a failing caused by a prior failing. Later, that same airline hired Ed in an administrative job, which became a stepping stone to eventually running his own airline. Had he succeeded on his first interview, he might have topped out as the head of an airline accounting department.

After Evander Holyfield knocked out Buster Douglas and became the heavyweight boxing champion, TV host Arsenio Hall asked Holyfield whether he was afraid of getting hurt when he entered the ring. Holyfield, who had never lost a fight, said, "I once got knocked down. I got up again, so I know it's not so bad."

That same attitude was expressed by Howard Ruff, the publisher of the Ruff Report and a proponent and teacher of entrepreneurship. Ruff lost everything about 20 years ago, when his Evelyn Wood Reading Dynamics business went under, sending him deep into debt. "At the time," he told me, "I was horribly bothered by it. But I decided not to let it drag me down, and over the years I got perspective and lost my fear of failure because I'd gone through it, recovered from it, and it wasn't the end of the world."

There was a time when failing in business meant you could never reenter the business community, never again walk with your head high. Those times have passed. We haven't come so far that the bankruptcy of major corporations or elegant stores, such as Bloomingdales, have made bankruptcy chic, but barring fraud, it's no longer the end of the world. A business failure won't make you feel as good as a success, but there is no permanent taint. That may be truer in the United States than elsewhere, not because we are less adept as entrepreneurs but because the U.S. culture encourages entrepreneurship and tolerates all its natural consequences, including the possibility, which is more remote than you may think, of a bankruptcy.

Profile

Barry Potekin: The Comeback Kid

The day Barry Potekin flunked fifth grade, his buddies jeered him all the way home, then dropped him like a bad habit. Barry was deeply humiliated, began hanging around with a bunch of idlers, and barely graduated from high school. After knocking around a bit, he landed in the rough-and-tumble world of commodity trading.

Barry's trading career started well. The atmosphere and personalities reminded him of his high school days. The best traders are tough, street-wise, and determined. Rude behavior is the norm. Fortunes are often won or lost in a few minutes of frenzied trading, so there's no time to observe the niceties. Barry quickly took to the business and made very good money in commodities during the early 1970s. But then came Jimmy Carter's presidency and its policies that drove commodity prices

down through the floor. Scores of traders were driven off
the floor; they were wiped out. Barry Potekin also lost
everything, including his parents' retirement money. One week
he savored $80 dinners, the next week his car was repossessed.

Barry and his father were both devastated. They met outside a
Bagel Nosh to have breakfast and to cry on each other's
shoulder. Each hoped the other had $2. But as it turned out, they
only had 80 cents between them. Barry remembers, "We went
in and split a bagel. He took the top half and I took the
bottom half, and we split one cup of coffee. My dad busted out
crying and said, 'our lives are ruined. I ruined my life, you ruined
your life, all is lost....' So I gave us a pep talk.
'We're going to make a comeback. We're going to jump off
the canvas, Dad. This is it, we're coming back.' We both
got excited and shot out of there like two Don Quixotes." In their
renewed enthusiasm, they temporarily forgot their rock-bottom
state. "The only thing we didn't have was an idea or money or
credit. We had bad credit," which didn't bother Barry. "Other than
that, we're coming back. This is it Dad..., we're coming back."

Someone had told him the way to make the most money fast
while investing the least was in fast food. None of it was true, he
says, but "God protects fools." He noticed the thousands of hot
dog stands and fast food places in Chicago. Realizing that
"you can't run with the herd," he looked for a hole in the market.
"In those days, there wasn't any upscale fast food. I saw a need
for a guy in a hurry who wants real food, and if it's an extra
fifty cents, I don't look at my change from a five, do you? I mean
if it's a little extra, who cares? I don't want that greasy, terrible-
looking hamburger."

Barry took his idea to banks and venture capitalists, but he got
nowhere. So he made a long list of friends and started
soliciting. "Eight hundred dollars, four hundred, two hundred...this
and that. Then I sold off a major hunk—one-fourth of the
business for $10,000, which I thought was reasonable, and to
make a long story short, we opened January 14, 1985...
nine dollars in the checking account and no food.

"I went to ten people who had already told me no and I
said, 'I'm asking tonight and tomorrow from ten people for
$10 apiece. Would you give me $10? And all ten gave it to me.

But do you know how they gave it to me? 'Get out of here, here's the ten, get away from me already.' You know, like a bum. But what am I going to do? I took it. I wanted to say, keep that ten, you know what I mean? I ran out and bought some hot dogs and hamburgers and chickens. The next morning it opened.

"Two hours later, we ran out of food. I took the money from the register and ran out for food and ran back. The first week, I was going two or three times a day for food, until I started to build it up. I had miscalculated everything. I had to raise the prices. I didn't know about food quantity. I didn't know anything. I went into this not knowing anything about the restaurant business and came within inches of going bankrupt the first six months. Then, sort of, the boat righted itself...."

Later, Barry knew that his Gold Coast Dogs was on its way when his mother called him one morning exclaiming, "We're in the newspapers." "What! I never took nothin'." "She says, 'No, you don't understand, you have the best hot dog in Chicago!'"

Barry Potekin's Secret Weapon

Barry is unlettered and probably unemployable, but he is definitely an entrepreneur. Nothing stands in the way of his dream, not even the humiliation of begging $10 from contemptuous friends. After wiping out his parents, he figured he needed to make three livings: "I needed a long shot. From going broke, from starting with no money and making a lot of money and then losing it, then bouncing around broke, inside me developed a tremendous desire to succeed. And I was willing to do whatever it took...so long as it was legal," he said. His secret weapon was an indomitable spirit that carried him past early setbacks in grade school, not to mention the trauma of losing the entire family nest egg in commodities.

"I've Never Met an Entrepreneur Who Is a Failure"

I've met entrepreneurs whose businesses have failed and whose projects have failed, but I've never met an entrepreneur who is a failure. The project that Thurman Rodgers introduced at American Microsystems was, according to him, "a pretty colossal failure" and was dropped. Microsystems dropped Rodgers, who tried to start his own business, but the effort failed. Rodgers had worked hard to learn how to finance and start a business and how to market in ways that American Microsystems had not. Those failures, he says, "didn't put a dent in my belief that one day I would run a company. It would work out. It happened that it didn't work out that day." How remarkable it is that those prior failures didn't cause Rodgers to call it quits. Why didn't they? Because only the projects failed, Rodgers didn't. He knew he'd eventually get it right.

Steve Brill refers to the process as the "testing of ideas." He told me, "We always try ideas that fail. I'm really proud of the fact that we started *Manhattan Lawyer,* which we later shut. It was the product of a really dumb idea, purely mine. If you don't do things that don't succeed, you won't do anything that really does succeed." Notice, also, how Brill didn't say he failed; the idea failed. Sure, it was his idea and it was dumb, but he didn't fail. In fact, he didn't even say the idea failed, he said it didn't succeed. Eyal Shavit, founder of Manof Systems, cofounder of new businesses, and mentor to many Israeli entrepreneurs, also says, "I didn't succeed to reach him by phone," not "I failed to reach him by phone." Because English is Eyal's second language, I thought at first that it was a linguistic difference. But I know many Israelis who say "I failed" and realized that Eyal was sending a meaningful message. Brill confirmed that.

Entrepreneurs don't aim to fail but do consider failing an acceptable, expected, natural occurrence. They view their failings as hash marks on the sleeve of their business uniform—a kind of decoration of valor—and they know that the more such hash marks they have, the better an entrepreneur they will be. Managers, however, fear that failing will mark not their sleeves but their corporate files. Managers worry that their failings will be deemed failures, stopping their ascent up the corporate ladder and barring their access to other corporations and ladders. Although entrepreneurs advance by experimenting and testing conventional boundaries, managers tend to be bound by precedent—some because they acquiesce, and some because their corporations insist upon it.

Fear of Failure as Terror

Karl Wallenda, the leader of the famous Flying Wallendas family trapeze act, was the foremost high-wire walker in the world. Wallenda walked wires between tall buildings without a net, thinking of nothing except walking the wire. Wallenda's wife said he never thought about falling. Then one night before a planned walk between hotel towers in Puerto Rico, he told his wife that, for the first time, he was thinking about falling. Next day, he fell to his death.

Thinking about falling led to Karl Wallenda's fall. That is what professors Namus and Benis call the "Wallenda Factor" in their book *Leaders*. The same is true for entrepreneurs. If you dwell on failing, you will fail.

Entrepreneurs are not super heroes. They fail; they have fears; and they even fear the possibility of failure. But the word "fear" has two meanings: fright and awe. Nonentrepreneurs may be so frightened of failing that it keeps them from trying. Entrepreneurs, however, see fear of failure as part of the process that leads to the goal of entrepreneurship. They respect that process, understand its downfalls, and are attracted to it like a bee to honey. They are not frightened of failing but are stimulated to chase their dream business.

President Franklin Delano Roosevelt's message that the only thing to fear is fear itself lifted our nation out of the Great Depression by addressing our collective fear about the economy (collective fear is where the economy's status causes all consumers to decrease their consumption, which will further dampen the economy). Collective fear is far more difficult to contemplate and comprehend than any fear you might encounter. So, following President Roosevelt's advice should be a snap for you and can lift you out of a minor depression and make you feel as if you are walking the high wire.

7

The Trap of
the Attractive Track

Gather ye rosebuds while ye may.
ROBERT HERRICK

Some people never build the business of their dreams because things are so good or so comfortable that they wouldn't dare risk what they have. Any employee who is satisfied with or afraid of losing the status quo probably fits this category, but the best examples are the executives who are continually promoted to higher levels of responsibility, authority, and compensation. All those people are on the attractive track, where they are blind to alternative opportunities. Only when the status quo is shaken and these executives fall off the attractive track does entrepreneurship become an attractive alternative.

Beware of Emotional
Premises

Unlike the first three emotionally driven reasons for leaving dreams unfulfilled (excuses, myths, and fear of failure), the attractive track is logically based. Its premise is that "a bird in the hand is worth two in the bush." In this case, you have a good job, and sacrificing it would be foolish.

"Bird in the hand" thinking is logical, but it's actually another trap because it is based on premises that are really rather emotional. For instance, your willingness to give up the bird in hand for the two in the bush depends on your drive and risk-aversion levels, which, in turn, depend upon feelings of confidence and self-esteem. So, what seems logical is actually based on emotional factors. The fact that the premises are emotional is all right, so long as you recognize the premises for what they are.

These premises are hard to see in ourselves and can blind us to opportunities that otherwise might interest us. If you're on an unattractive track, nothing prevents you from jumping off to grab a brass ring when it's within reach. However, if you're on the attractive track, the blindness becomes almost total. It's just too hard to give up a good thing, especially when the alternative is so little known. Well-rewarded executives who might consider entrepreneurial alternatives have it worst of all. They must determine whether the bird in the hand is as secure or satisfying as you think. Simple insight may be all you need to rebalance your scale.

When Art Fry, an employee of 3M Company, created the yellow, stick-to-anything note pads called Post-its, he received a promotion and a generous salary increase. He was also elected to the Carlton Society, which Art referred to as 3M's equivalent of the Nobel prize. Post-its have made 3M a fortune, and Art Fry is on everyone's list of intrapreneurs. But Art Fry didn't make a fortune and doesn't fit most definitions of an entrepreneur.

I asked Art Fry why he didn't create the Post-it business on his own. He told me he had a contract with 3M that precluded such entrepreneurship, but, even if he had been free to pursue his idea on his own, he would not have done so. He felt that his idea could succeed only with the financial, research, distribution, sales, and marketing support 3M could give it. Because 3M had developed an environment that satisfied Art Fry's needs, the company made Art Fry's track so attractive to him that he would never consider leaving. Art is now 60 years old. Retirement is just a few years off. He thinks that after he retires he just might try something different, perhaps as an entrepreneur.

In many countries, it is extremely difficult for employees to see the ruts in their tracks; indeed, some societies pressure employees not to question their corporate careers. In the United States, however, there is a force that urges people to break from their attractive tracks and start their own businesses. Americans respect self-made entrepreneurs much more than they respect managers of large companies. We revere the trailblazer who has the guts to forge new paths. Although big salaries and perks keep some managers on the attractive track, the force—derived from society's respect and recognition—enables, even causes, a disproportionate number of U.S. managers to jump from the track and become entrepreneurs.

How to Get Off the Attractive Track

Indy drivers go around the track, lap after lap, in cars that can steer in only one direction—left. There is no point in looking at alternative directions, as long as the race is going well. As the race goes on, the heat of tire friction makes the track very smooth—almost like glass—and the cars lose their much needed traction. Good drivers edge up the outer track wall to get "tack" (softer, stickier asphalt) on their slick tires. The attractive track in business is more like the rut in a well-worn path. Executives continue on their established ways, lap after lap. The more laps they do, the deeper the rut becomes. They don't need tack. They're not slipping.

These executives are happy with their support system, comfortably in the groove. This is the attractive track until outside forces intervene. Commitments to family may prevent another relocation that is a prerequisite to the next ladder rung. Jobs may be cut in a restructuring, for example, pushing executives completely off the track. The corporate exit decision has been made for them, at least temporarily. When this happens, however, often the entrepreneurs among them don't try to reenter the corporate world. Instead, they forsake the attractive track forever.

Phil Matthews had spent a lifetime on the attractive track. He was high school valedictorian, top of his college class, top honors at Harvard Business School, a coveted first position at Chrysler, constant promotions there, stolen by Pepsi, where increasing responsibilities and titles flowed, and, finally, an offer by Dart to be number-two man. With corporate America polishing Phil's track, there was no need to even contemplate alternatives to such smooth sailing.

Each company change and many title changes had required a relocation. Phil's wife, daughter, and son had had enough when Dart's offer meant another move to California. Phil promised them that it would be their last move. Then Dart merged with Chicago-based Kraft. Phil was now a top dog at a gigantic company, so for a year or so, Phil commuted from Chicago to California. Finally, to ensure control over his choice of domicile, he jumped from his attractive track and bought Bell Helmet Co., where he has prospered and stayed put.

Mary Anne Jackson had been a consultant at accounting firms before she got a fast-track job at Beatrice Foods. In relatively few years and at a lower management level, she gained valuable experience in strategic planning, turnarounds, project management, new product development, and operations. It didn't matter to Mary Anne whether the business belonged to Beatrice, belonged to another company, or belonged to her, so long as she would be running it. Her only goal was to run a business. She was so new on the attractive track that she never thought about leaving that track or even changing vehicles.

One day, Mary Anne Jackson's track didn't just get slippery, it downright fell out from under her. When Beatrice gave her notice, she had to make a change. She could have just changed employers, but the forced change awakened her and prompted her to look at other alternatives. Mary Anne decided to become her new employer.

Profile

Mary Anne Jackson: Networking for Fun and Profit

Even though Mary Anne Jackson was in an attractive track groove prior to Kohlberg Kravis Roberts & Co. buying the company, in reality, she was already bumping up against the glass ceiling at Beatrice Foods. A driven and talented executive, Mary Anne stepped on toes and bruised some male egos.
When KKR took over Beatrice, Mary Anne was an obvious target of its downsizing campaign, and she got the axe.

But Mary Anne was not concerned. She weighed her next move deliberately. She'd always wanted to run a company and figured now was the time. Before she was fired, she says she had a sudden epiphany when she realized that she wanted to develop her own product and use it to build a company. She then began weighing many possible ideas and finally came up with one that made sense.

As a working mother, she had worried about leaving her youngsters with a baby-sitter. Some baby-sitters fed the children cookies and even catsup sandwiches. Mary Anne tried to overcome this problem by cooking ahead and preparing a week's worth of meals for the freezer.

With millions of other mothers working to add to family income, she figured they'd welcome wholesome, quick-serve meals for their kids. She targeted children left with baby-sitters as well as latch key kids who had to fend for themselves. Her ambitious plan called for national distribution of ready-to-eat dinners. She realized that inevitably she'd be asking for competition from some of the most competitive concerns in the world: Hormel, Chef Boyardee, and Kraft Foods.

Mary Anne tested the concept first with a careful survey of 2000 parents in the Chicago area. (She distributed the survey through a diaper service that would do it for far less cost than a mailing.) Recruiting one of her out-placement colleagues to tabulate the results electronically, Mary Anne's survey showed that about 15 percent of the parents responded positively to the product concept. They also indicated what they wanted in the product—turkey and chicken over beef. No hot dogs, no MSG. The survey suggested the meals would sell at under $3 each at the supermarket.

Mary Anne then contacted friends, former associates, and food industry acquaintances. She also turned to the out-placement office, milking it for lots of free advice, willingly offered. Even more advice was wangled through barter deals with a number of sympathetic top industry pros, many of whom had been laid off too. With their help and with the project knowledge she gained at Beatrice, she set up and organized My Own Meals—acronym *MOM*.

Though Mary Anne ran the show, dozens of people were

involved. Obviously, big company managers aren't experts in
every stage of new-product creation. Mary Anne was no
exception. Start-up entrepreneurs develop hands-on expertise as
they go along. Mary Anne found herself suddenly wearing the
hats of planner, conceptualizer, expediter, critic, cheerleader, and
decision maker. Rather than go it alone, she used outside
specialists to shore up her expertise during each step of the
endeavor. Unpaid creative pros, for instance, designed
the product and the packaging. She called on marketing and
packaging experts still at Beatrice and other professionals
she knew at Kraft. She also called specialists she'd met at trade
shows. She used her corporate connections to find a job for
another unpaid professional.

Entrepreneurs who do not come from the corporate culture are
usually less willing to ask for help. But Mary Anne had the self-
confidence to use outsiders and to believe that she could sort the
good advice from the bad. She accepted the fact that someone
else could have an idea worth pursuing or a technique
worth trying. Also, she returned the favor. For example, she
named one unpaid woman assistant a vice president to spruce up
the woman's résumé.

With all the free help, she managed to limit expenses to a
remarkable degree. Package design cost her $37,000; product
development cost $60,000; office expenses and travel
another $40,000; and her assistant's salary was roughly $30,000.
Mary Anne did not collect a salary for her own services
during the start-up phase.

Very few executives are as versatile and well-connected as
Mary Anne Jackson. She financed her venture with private
offerings of stock, and she sold her investors *personally.* Her first
offering was completed in May of 1987. With it, she raised
$365,000. Most of the 22 investors were former food industry
executives, including people from Beatrice, Kraft, and
Quaker Oats—along with a few doctors.

Mary Anne did so well with My Own Meals that the major
food processors soon designed similar products of their own. She
lost a major distributor in Jewel Food Stores and has suffered a
number of other setbacks. She told me that if for some reason she
couldn't go on with MOM, she would simply start another

business. Why? "Because I have another idea. Once you get started, you have all these ideas. There are so many things that need to be accomplished in this world." If and when she does begin another business, there is one thing you can count on. Mary Anne will use her contacts very effectively.

Mary Anne Jackson's Secret Weapon: Down-to-Earth Practicality

While Mary Anne Jackson was still at Beatrice Foods, the company hired a former partner in a consulting firm. Several colleagues said, "Wow. Isn't she smart!" Mary Anne said, "Why do you think she's so smart? What has she accomplished?" And they said, "Well, she's a Harvard MBA." Mary Anne, a pragmatist at heart, came back with, "That just means she can study and afford it. That doesn't mean that she can accomplish anything. Wait until she accomplishes something, and then you can come back to me and tell me how smart she is."

Mary Anne remembered a Beatrice turnaround she worked on where only one salesperson actually showed rising sales. He was getting new accounts, too. And his yearly sales were up even without the new business. He had also improved his margins.

Mary Anne asked the salesperson to take someone with him on sales calls so that in case he left the company, the apprentice could take up the slack.

The man did something that no one had ever done to Mary Anne before:

> He looked me straight in the eye and said, "Babe, let me tell you something. That's my insurance. I'm not going to give you all my secrets."
>
> After we both finally calmed down, he got me on his wavelength and I got him on my wavelength, we sat down and we talked. What I learned from him was phenomenal. Sales were a function of helping other people solve their problems.
>
> What he did with me was show me how he was able to accomplish the kinds of things he could do. Now this guy

had a high school education at best. Yet, he was very successful within his own environment and in the business where he
operated.

If I put him side by side with this woman who had a
Harvard MBA, she would fail miserably because she did not
know how to get things done by working in a business environment. She could sit back and analyze the company like I
did and evaluate what was wrong, but she would not necessarily know how to go fix it.

That's because she wouldn't find a guy like this and say,
"All right, you are probably better than I am. You tell me
how we should fix it." Without the advantage of his experience, she'd do it wrong.

Profile

Phillip Matthews Goes for Broke

If you are thinking about setting up a business but hate to give
up your secretary, free photocopies, the rest of the corporate
services, and your medical and other employee benefits, imagine
what it would be like to give up the corporate jet and the other
lush perks of high office and then put your house and your
life savings on the line.

No one I've met has been more cozily situated than Phillip
Matthews. Corporate America was Phillip Matthews's natural
haunt. After getting his MBA at Harvard Business School, Phillip
went to Detroit, first to get his hands dirty in a factory job at
Chrysler and eventually to become controller of a major division
at age 27. Early power, authority, and responsibility were
intoxicating. He "grabbed the brass ring," leaving to be vice
president of finance at a $200 million unit of conglomerate Gulf &
Western Industries. Expanded power of position satisfied his
ego and his economic needs. He left Gulf & Western to join
Pepsico's Wilson Sporting Goods unit. He was put in charge of
operations—manufacturing, purchasing, and the rest—and
was later tapped to do the same thing for Pepsi's Frito Lay, as
senior vice president of operations, where he commanded 40
factories. By now, the corner office carried with it the perks and
trappings of corporate power.

When his former boss at Wilson became president of Dart Industries, he asked Matthews to become his chief of staff, Phillip's first corporate staff job ever. In time, he became executive vice president and chief financial officer of this $2 billion company. Phillip not only had a corner office but now it was located on the executive floor. Dart merged with Kraft, and Phillip became chief financial officer of the $10 billion enterprise headquartered in Chicago. That made Phillip one of the most powerful CFOs in the country, and he enjoyed commensurate financial rewards. All this career success caused some personal stress. Phillip's quick ascent had necessitated many relocations, which disrupted his family life. Earlier, when Phillip uprooted his wife and moved her to California, he told her he'd never do it again. So when the Dart and Kraft merger relocated him to Chicago from California, he commuted for over a year rather than move again.

Phillip Matthews had no wish to go the entrepreneurial route, but he was bent on controlling his life. It was especially important to him that he play a significant role in his children's lives. So when he bailed out to become a one-third partner in a leveraged buy-out of Bell Helmets, his commitment to his family was complete.

He joined that "private, noncorporate world" in 1980, as a principle owner of the company that made helmets for three sports businesses: auto racing, motorcycling, and bicycling. There, he found that, "for the first time, many of my decisions were motivated by personal things rather than career things." As a part-owner of a business, he was in control.

Phillip now had more time for his family. He renewed ties with his son, going off alone with him for a week or two. They did Outward Bound projects a couple of times. They learned how to race cars, and these two nongolfers went to Scotland and Ireland to golf for a week together. They even took a fly-fishing trip, something they had never done before.

Phillip's positive family experience more than compensated for the corporate social status he lost. By taking the entrepreneurial route, Phillip's expectations of a better balance between work and family were satisfied. He was surprised, though, by other aspects of his new entrepreneurial life. The big shock was,

as he puts it, "the risk-taking requirement." "Bell Helmets
was losing money and that's how I could get involved without
having a great capital base. [But] the problem of making a payroll
and having your house on the line, and a lot of the cash you
worked hard all your life to put in the bank and see it on
the line...was a very difficult thing for me for a couple of years."

Matthews was not, perhaps, a born entrepreneur. But when
corporate life threatened his home life, he decided to go for
broke. He left the attractive track, protected only by his
Bell helmet. His motivation to succeed was, in a very real sense,
as strong as any entrepreneur's.

Get Tack on Your Tires

First, make sure you know what it means to leave the attractive
track. The compensation and perks are easy to measure and difficult to abandon. Some sacrifices are less apparent. Many entrepreneurs who left an attractive track note that the biggest shock
to their system was not having their calls answered. They no
longer enjoyed the clout of their position and their big company.
Consider the supplier or banker to whom your call had been a
command performance, perhaps because your company's business had been very important to them. Suddenly, they take days
to respond to your call as an independent entrepreneur.

Second, keep or put yourself in shape for making the sprint
off the track. If you are burdened with large mortgages or other
debts or even high fixed expenses, such as car leases, country
club dues and charges, vacation home, and social commitments,
including entertainment, clothing, and travel, the "security" of
your paycheck may be more like a maximum security prison.
Joe Sullivan, the former president of Swift, talked about the
need to be in a financial position to give entrepreneurial opportunities fair consideration.

Third, talk with others who have left the attractive track.
Remember, their calls aren't being answered as much, so they'll
welcome your call. That doesn't mean they're not busy; all
entrepreneurs have too much to do. However, entrepreneurs
find time for what's important. Most would welcome an oppor-

tunity to reflect on what they have accomplished. Consider carefully how they made the break, but also hear how they feared doing so and what got them over the hump. Your facts may differ, but you can use their example to motivate you.

Fourth, take the time to analyze what is really important to you. How vital is it for you to determine your own destiny? Must you do so to demonstrate your ability to perform and accomplish, to realize a fair return on your personal investment, or to satisfy your obligations to your family and yourself as a social being?

8
Risk

It was a risk I had to take and took.

ROBERT FROST

Risk is real, and all entrepreneurs must deal with it. However, risk is by no means exclusive to entrepreneurs. Other people—police officers, fire fighters, soldiers, and high-rise construction workers—bear risks that are greater and more constant.

Risk or a willingness to deal with risk alone does not make one an entrepreneur, but how and why one deals with risk might. If you understand why and how to deal with risk, you'll find doing so easy. Advice from the entrepreneurs I interviewed can't eliminate your risks, but it can show you how to deal with them.

What Do Entrepreneurs Risk?

If all you risk is your existing job, are you an entrepreneur? I think so, but not all entrepreneurs agree. Edson de Castro left Digital Equipment Corporation to found Data General Corporation. He told me, "I've got a somewhat warped view of what risk is or isn't. At the end of the day, if your venture fails, you're not going to be dead or in jail. You're going to have another job, and it's probably going to be OK. It's all a question of the magnitude." At certain times and for certain people, the magnitude may seem greater than for others. Either way, the risk inherent in leaving your existing job is sufficient to qualify you as an entrepreneur.

However, according to Lester Crown, to be called an entrepreneur you must have a part of your net worth at risk in a business. Lester Crown, whose net worth is measured in billions, says it doesn't matter how much you invest, as long as it constitutes a significant portion of what you have. Without that level of financial commitment, you won't have what Lester refers to as the essence of entrepreneurs, "their heart pumping real hard." He doesn't think the risk level must be great; he encourages risk reduction whenever possible. Risk level, however, relates to the degree of risk—the probabilities—and has nothing to do with the amount or percentage of wealth at risk.

For entrepreneurs, wealth isn't the only measurable thing at risk. Don Jacobs told me he considers himself an entrepreneur because he built the business known as Northwestern's Kellogg School from nothing to the best there is. His only investments in the school are his soul and his sweat, which don't even translate into "sweat equity," because Northwestern, not Don, owns Kellogg. Of course, the traditionally low compensation that educators receive causes them to trade in the special currency issued by the State of Academia, namely academic pride, which Don surely invested in large measure as he built Kellogg.

People who risk such special currencies, such as pride, in pursuit of their dreams are also entrepreneurs.

The Only Entrepreneurs in Las Vegas Own the Casinos

When people gamble, trade, or speculate, there is a balance—between all the winners on the one hand and all the losers on the other hand. You may not know specifically who is gambling or trading on the other side, but the sum of all the winnings must equal the sum of all the losings. Gambling and trading are "win-lose" situations. In entrepreneurship, that is not so. Entrepreneurs can engage in win-win situations, where everyone wins because entrepreneurs are economically productive, can create jobs for workers, profits for suppliers, and opportunities for customers. So entrepreneurship is less risky than gambling, trading, or speculating.

The quantity of risk is not the only difference. Gamblers, traders, and speculators view risk differently than do entrepreneurs. To gamblers, traders, and speculators, risk is an end; to entrepreneurs, risk is a means.

Are Franchisees Entrepreneurs?

Manpower is the largest temporary help agency in the world, but it was once a small venture that was run, part-time, by two Milwaukee practicing lawyers who had trouble finding temp secretaries, assumed others had similar problems, and set out to fill the need. When Elmer Winter and Aaron Scheinfeld, the founders of Manpower, wanted to expand, they decided to franchise new agencies. Eventually, Elmer Winter became president of the International Franchise Association.

Winter, who retired from Manpower about 20 years ago, said his franchisees back then were all entrepreneurs. "They borrowed money...to pay initial franchise fees and...meet the payroll. They had everything they owned [in the business]. Their mothers and fathers helped out [as employees. Those franchisees] worked very hard."

Don Boroian, founder of Francorp, the biggest franchise consulting firm, thinks that all franchisees are entrepreneurs. I think Boroian is correct. Granted, certain well-established franchisors, through their increased guidelines and support, may offer potential franchisees a much-reduced level of risk than some start-up franchisor. As a result, their franchisees may have fewer options and less control. Some franchisors actually advertise that buying their franchise is less risky than starting your own business. Then how can Boroian be right? Watch out! You're falling into a trap again. The test of whether someone is an entrepreneur is neither that they bear the highest levels of risk nor that they have absolute control.

The extreme example of the franchise with the least risk and flexibility is McDonald's. Although the early McDonald's franchisees, who bought from a start-up named Ray Kroc, assumed a big risk and had something to say about how their restaurants were run, getting a McDonald's franchise today is viewed as a sure thing and includes a commitment to abide by McDonald's rules, which are geared to consistently applying proven programs. There doesn't seem to be much room to "do your own thing."

Are McDonald's franchisees still entrepreneurs? You bet they are! Neither control nor risk must meet quantitative absolutes to constitute entrepreneurship. Although rare, some McDonald's franchisees do fail; some others make less than they could; and individual effort does make a difference. To start, a McDonald's franchisee must agree with the selection of location—perhaps the three most important decisions—even though it is generally chosen and secured by McDonald's. Within limits, decor, service, and public relations can be enhanced by individual franchisees to improve their business and results. The fact that McDonald's watches carefully and almost always suggests improvements before it's too late only affects the quantitative aspect of a franchisee's involvement. The franchisees can change, for better or for worse, the nerve center of their business, however slight such change may seem, and thus even McDonald's franchisees are entrepreneurs.

Entrepreneurs and Managers Handle Risk Differently

Everyone who runs a business must deal with risks and rewards. Edson de Castro feels that entrepreneurs might have a "warped view of what risk is" because they frequently don't think they are taking risks when nonentrepreneurs think they are. Managers, however, according to de Castro, are supposed to get rid of or reduce risk.

Ned Heizer founded and ran Allstate Insurance's venture capital division, where he backed more than 70 entrepreneurs' companies, such as Teledyne, Amdahl, and International House of Pancakes, with an overall return to Allstate of over 46 percent per year. His division used less than 4 percent of Allstate's capital and generated more than half their earnings. After Ned left Allstate, he founded the Heizer Corporation and later the Heizer Center for Entrepreneurship at Northwestern University's Kellogg School.

Ned believes that business schools teach students to avoid risk and that big companies build the avoidance of risk into their management structure. He says that the analyses of both are limited to risk analysis and that "no one is paid to take risks." He believes that the Japanese managers, despite their cultural reluctance to lose face, are less risk-averse than U.S. managers and spend more time analyzing how to get something done, rather than worrying about what to do if you fail.

To understand how professional managers and entrepreneurs handle risk differently, imagine that they each have two PCs in front of them. One PC's screen lists all the risks, and the other PC's screen lists all the rewards. The managers keep both screens in front of them all the time—forever. Entrepreneurs quickly put the screen listing all the risks behind them, so they can focus on the rewards.

Howard Schultz, the founder of Starbucks, the extraordinarily successful coffee store chain, has a slightly different metaphor: As though driving a car, he views opportunity through the front windshield and risk in the rearview mirror. He constantly drives forward and keeps his eye on the opportunities, though he looks in the rearview mirror, from time to time, to be aware of risks.

To entrepreneurs, risk is merely one factor in the equation; risk is a flashing yellow traffic light that you glance at as you whiz by on the highway of business. To managers, however, risk is a barrier; risk is a flashing red traffic light that you keep your eyes on and that makes you stop. Risk is real, but perceptions of it vary, as do the ways people relate to and deal with risk, somewhat because of the passion with which entrepreneurs view the equation's other factors.

Jerry Rogers puts it somewhat differently, "I am not one that looks over my shoulder. The issue is what's in front of me, the opportunities or challenges in front of me. That's the excitement."

Evaluate What's Really at Risk

Jack Miller, the founder of Quill, told me that, despite his lack of savings and his need to support his young family, he gave up his job to start Quill out of his in-laws' home and the trunk of his car. He wasn't concerned about the job; he knew he could always get another one.

Suppose you don't share Jack Miller's nerve, and you tell yourself, "I can't afford to lose my job or our savings, if the new business goes bad." You further conclude that, if you can't afford the risk, you should not take it. That conclusion is what you got by evaluating the excuse. Remember, instead, to evaluate the components. As Edson de Castro said, the risk "is all a question of the magnitude." Evaluate whether you really can afford the risk. If you lost your job, how long would it take to get a new one and rise to your present level? Your loss of pay until you get a job and your difference in pay until you achieve the same level is your actual risk. Isn't that risk far less intimidating than the overwhelming concept of "losing your job"? Remember, also, to evaluate whether you like your job and how much you want to be your own boss.

Evaluate the potential reward as well as the potential risk. Whether you can afford the risk depends not only on how much the risk costs and its likelihood of occurring but also on the possible benefit. The reward doesn't reduce the risk, but it may make the risk worthwhile. Evaluate both and their interrelationship.

Try this exercise. If your original excuse is:

I can't afford to lose my job if the business goes bad.

change your excuse to:

If I lose my job, it will take me two months to find a new one and six months to attain my present level. That total cost is $_____. If the business goes well, I can make a fortune, and, since I don't like my job anymore, taking the risk seems acceptable.

Point of Information

Is Money the Real Risk?

Just as entrepreneurs aren't "in it" for the money, which
generally is merely a measuring stick, the risk of becoming an
entrepreneur isn't the money they might lose. Anyway,
these days, the money invested in most entrepreneurial ventures
doesn't belong to the entrepreneurs. The street of dreams is
paved with other people's money ("OPM"). Therefore, as
an entrepreneur, you must learn how to deal with the investment
community, which has both great diversity (e.g., commercial
lenders, mezzanine financiers, angels, venture capitalists, private
placement brokers, public offering underwriters) and, yet,
certain common characteristic concerns.

Investors are not going to buy into your dream unless they are
convinced that you are realistic about your business prospects.
If you speak of a sure thing, you may elicit the typical response to
a "trust me" approach. They weren't born yesterday. Be
enthusiastic, but be prepared to back your enthusiasm with a
track record or other convincing argument.

You may not have a track record of starting your own
company, but maybe you did something at work that shows the
right stuff. Art Fry has always been an employee of a large
corporation; he has never founded, owned, or run his
own company. Yet, I assure you that Art could generate the
necessary support for a new venture. The large corporation Art
worked for was Minnesota Mining and Manufacturing (3M)
where he invented Post-its. But Art didn't just invent 3M's
second biggest selling product. When management couldn't see
the potential of Post-its, he began using them in ways that
fellow employees would notice—as book markers, reminders,
message slips, and even as instruction notations on song books
for the company choir. He found dozens of ways to use the
markers and finally persuaded management to take on what has
become a $200 million business for the innovative 3M
corporation.

"Oh, sure," you say, "show them the last time I invented and raised money for this widget or any other widget. This is my first time out of the starting gate. I have no track record. That's why I'm reading this book."

Remember, though, that life consists of many tracks. You have probably raced along several of them but don't realize their relevance to your unique entrepreneurial undertaking. You may have demonstrated your ability to succeed while working as an employee, volunteering for charitable or civic organizations, or running your household. For example, you might review the special project you undertook on your own as an employee to develop a new product or explain how you set up an environmental task force and what it accomplished.

Of course, investors would prefer to see a track record in business; that's easier to compare. However, what they are really looking for is what you are made of, and your job is to demonstrate the relevance of your track record, whatever its essence. For example, hundreds of homemakers have discovered that the skills they developed running a household are transferable to a business situation, similarly if they have organized church picnics or run the PTA.

Potential investors are going to ask you why you don't raise at least some of the money from your personal assets. They may ask if you have a second mortgage or if you have sold valuable personal property—your summer home and/or your securities.

Fair questions. Be prepared to answer them. Investors need assurance that you are committed to your dream, because if you don't buy it, then why should they?

You should tell them that you are risking your reputation, your ego, and your time while closing doors to alternative opportunities. Make sure the investors understand this. Explain that you are totally committed to this dream, it is in the very fiber of your being. When they ask why you don't stake your house and family heirlooms, it is because they need reassurance—that you are in fact committed to the project. Do everything you can to convince them you have no diversions. (Remember, one dream at a time. Whatever you do, don't parade your other ideas before them.) Be sure you convince them this is your future, that you are in this for the long haul.

You should also explain that the best way for them to keep

your mind on the business is to help protect your assets. An entrepreneur who is concerned about losing everything is hardly focused in the right direction. There are better ways to evidence your commitment. This isn't a test of machismo. Nor does having everything at risk ensure commitment. Actually, enduring such risk may cause judgments that investors wouldn't want their entrepreneur to make.

Venture capital is its own special brand of OPM and breeds a unique reaction from some entrepreneurs. People don't like someone looking over their shoulders. It follows naturally that relations between venture capitalist and entrepreneur can be touchy, even difficult. During the Vietnam war, I had a client who derisively referred to his venture capitalists as "the VC," which, of course, was also used as an abbreviation for the Viet Cong.

The VC are not necessarily the enemy. Let's face it, if you put your money in someone else's business, you would have more than a passing interest in how well the entrepreneur was using your capital. And so it is with venture capitalists. But contrary to widely held beliefs, venture capitalists are not just marking time waiting for you to screw up so they can seize your baby. That can happen—don't be fooled. But that isn't the grand scheme at all. Rest assured, the venture capitalist needs your talents at work.

The typical venture capitalist has 15 to 20 deals perking at one time. He or she is also looking at another 15 to 20 deals at the same time. The last thing the capitalist needs is to have to run somebody else's business indefinitely. The circumstances are akin to the bank that forecloses on a private home. The bank doesn't want to be in real estate management because it isn't structured to do this work. Nor is the venture capitalist set up to run your business. The venture capitalist really wants you to succeed. After all, the business is your dream. As the entrepreneur, you see it better than anyone else. The venture capitalist bet on you. When a venture capitalist drops an entrepreneur, both have failed in their roles. Everything considered, the capitalist is aware that it would be counterproductive to try to control or stifle your business. So concentrate on your dream. Don't focus on who is controlling whom.

9

The Entrepreneur's Work Ethic

None of the secrets of success will work unless you do.

A fortune cookie

Asking entrepreneurs and nonentrepreneurs what *work* means didn't prove enlightening, because work means something different to each person. But I got some interesting responses to this question: "What is the opposite of work to you?" Many people answer that question with words like "rest" or "play." Not entrepreneurs. Harold Geneen thought the opposite of work was sleep. Meanwhile, Jovan Trboyevic, a restauranteur, works in an industry where hard work generally is aimed at survival. Jovan answered my question indirectly by saying, "what comes between work is procrastination." Meaning that for entrepreneurs who consider work their whole life, anything else is a digression or interruption from the dominant, indeed only, goal. The ultimate response, though, was by Eileen Ford, founder of the Ford Model Agency, who said the opposite of work was death.

What's a Work Ethic?

Larry Levy, founder of the Levy Organization (which operates food services in places as diverse as Disney World, Chicago's McCormick Place Convention Center, and White Sox Park), is working on a joint venture with Steven Spielberg for a theater operation. Levy told me a story about his grandfather, an entrepreneur who owned a shoe repair shop, that I think explains the dual aspects of the entrepreneurial work ethic: how you apply yourself and how much you apply yourself to your work. One day in 1941, a man came to Larry's grandfather's shop and left a pair of shoes to be resoled. Unbeknownst to Larry's grandfather, the man was then drafted and served in the Army. After the War, he came back to the shop to pick up his shoes. Larry's grandfather told him, "They'll be ready next Tuesday." Larry's grandfather had an entrepreneurial work ethic, even though he put off work.

Hard work is not what entrepreneurs share in common. Some work very hard; others don't. They do, however, share a work ethic. An ethic is a guideline or code that tells you how to lead a portion of your life. A work ethic tells you how much to apply yourself. Although ethics are formed by the teachings and examples of others, ultimately ethics are stored within and a little voice inside tells you how much to apply yourself, prevents you from drifting from your goals, and lets you retain control over your work life.

Where Does a Work Ethic Come From?

The germ of a work ethic is in every person, including you, and it is molded by the myriad of people whose influences you feel. Of course, you are the one who accepts or rejects those influences, so ultimately you must bear the responsibility for your work ethic.

In general, your work ethic is formed very early in life. You may apply it, for years, in rather nonentrepreneurial ways, but that doesn't alter the essence of the work ethic, only its application. Joe Sullivan, the Esmark turnaround expert who delayed becoming an entrepreneur until he was almost 50, was raised in the Brighton section of Boston.

At the time, Brighton was populated almost entirely by the Irish and Jews. Both ethnic groups were scorned by the so-called Yankees who made it extremely difficult for the Irish and Jews to enter the finer schools and secure the better jobs. Joe told me that he learned early that "if you were Irish or Jewish, you had to work a hell of a lot harder and be a hell of a lot better than the so-called Yankees. It was drilled into me from a very early point that, in order to succeed, you had to be 25 percent better than the others. That was told to me by my parents and by the Jewish neighbors/businessmen who talked with me. It was a sort of collective wisdom from two diverse groups. That, in our neighborhood, was the work ethic." That collective wisdom that Joe adopted and that told him how hard to work was Joe's work ethic.

For some, it's sufficient to have a work ethic of doing just what is needed to get by; for others, the ethic demands whatever is required to get ahead. Whatever your work ethic, the important thing to know is that you can change your work ethic. You can make your work ethic more entrepreneurial.

Sometimes that something inside you is put there by your parents. Sam LeFrak told me that he came home from school one day and said to his mother, "Listen, I'm second in my class." She said, "Stop strutting like a peacock. You have still got one to beat." If your parents gave you that work ethic, all you have to do is follow it. If they didn't, then you may have to develop it, which isn't that hard if you know what to do.

Richie Melman, the founder of Lettuce Entertain You, a company that develops, owns, and operates dozens of successful restaurants, feels that his father was his predominant influence. He said, "I sometimes think that most terrific entrepreneurs have had an odd relationship with their fathers." Richie did. His father was picky, not generally very giving, and unable to give Richie the recognition he needed. Richie said, "I think I needed to show him, over and over and over again." (After his father died, Richie's mother told him that his father always raved to others about how he respected Richie's accomplishment.) Larry Levy also spoke about his father's influence, and Larry too spoke of his need to show his father, perhaps even after he was gone.

But Larry noted, "Everything I did for years was aimed at the approval of my father, which was the wrong reason, because in life you should please yourself. When he died, I realized that I was running as fast as I could to please him and all of a sudden I started to enjoy myself—both the doing and the achieving."

Sometimes the parental influence is less direct. Jenny Craig, the founder of the chain of diet centers bearing her name, told how her father carried as many as three jobs at a time as she grew up during the Depression. Her mother worried about him working so hard, so he'd say, "Hard work never killed anybody." Jenny grew up thinking that working hard ensured long life. Jenny's hard work led to achievement which proved gratifying. What began as a concern for long life became a confidence-building experience through success, achievement, and fulfillment.

Nor is it always the father's influence that is key. Eileen Ford said, "I always knew that I would work because my mother told me I would work. When I grew up, you believed your mother. She went to work when she was 13 and worked until she was 78." Phil Klutznick, former U.S. Secretary of Commerce and a very successful entrepreneur, also spoke of his mother as the work ethic influence in his life.

The initial seed of your work ethic may have been planted by a parent but, as you nurture the seed's growth, the work ethic that blooms is your own. Sam LeFrak is a known and accomplished doer in many areas. He not only built over a hundred thousand apartments but discovered Barbra Streisand and Eddie Murphy and helped find and raise the Titanic. He is sought after by local, federal, and foreign government officials, as well as by financiers, builders, landowners, and many others. LeFrak asked "What makes Sammy run?" and replied that he does, "Because everyone is chasing him."

The Protestant Work Ethic

"He who makes money pleases God." No, neither Martin Luther nor Norman Vincent Peale made that statement (nor did Ayn Rand, Milton Friedman, or Gordon Gecho, Michael Douglas's character in *Wall Street*). The quote comes from Mohammed. I doubt that Mohammed intended to promote profit for its own sake, just as I doubt that God cares about material wealth. But commitment, self-sacrifice, and productivity—how we use our time and our money—are the really important elements. They constitute our work ethic, which to God, Mohammed, Protestants, and entrepreneurs, whatever their religions, is far more important than making money.

Holly Hunt, founder of one of the most prominent showrooms in Chicago's Merchandise Mart, talked about the Protestant work ethic in connection with the entrepreneurial work ethic. Although Holly might be influenced by both of her grandfathers having been ministers, the Protestant work ethic actually has become nondenominational. Whatever your religion, subscribing to the Protestant work ethic means working hard and long. I think it also connotes working hard and long for the sake of working hard and long. Maybe it was called the Protestant work ethic because if you worked hard and long, you would be too busy to sin. I'm reminded of the observation by H. L. Mencken that a Puritan is not against bullfighting because of the pain it gives the bull but because of the pleasure it gives the spectators.

Entrepreneurs would never work for the sake of working. They work toward goals—very specific goals.

The Farmers' Work Ethic

Evelyn Echols, founder of the largest school for the travel industry, was raised on a farm where she developed a special work ethic by observing her father. American farmers are a perfect example of entrepreneurs. They own their farms, and their every working hour seems committed to making their farms productive. The first word they learn is *chores,* and chores become the keynote of their existence. They awake before the roosters and work into the evening. They may not seem as intent on building or expanding their business as do industrial and commercial entrepreneurs, perhaps because, for many, survival is the goal, whereas others share the continual dream that next year will be better. The farm is often their only tangible possession, yet they willingly mortgage it all for one of the riskiest businesses in history.

Farmers believe in working long and hard. They must, in order to compete with the elements of nature. Incidentally, they also don't subscribe to the conventional Protestant work ethic; instead, they work hard to achieve very specific goals.

Are Entrepreneurs Workaholics?

A popular image of entrepreneurs is that of a Jack (or Jill)-of-all-trades, with sleeves rolled up, covering all the bases, compulsively burning the candle at both ends to get everything done. To most people that sounds a lot like a workaholic, and they assume that workaholism is part of the entrepreneurs' work ethic.

Workaholism is an addiction, much like drug addiction, alcoholism, and gambling addictions. Drug addicts, alcoholics, and addicted gamblers tend to deny their affliction. Many entrepreneurs work every bit as hard as workaholics. However, I don't find that entrepreneurs deny how much they work; they actually brag about it. That distinction convinced me that hard-working entrepreneurs are not all workaholics.

The addiction of workaholics is work. The addiction of entrepreneurs is their dreams. To entrepreneurs, work is but the means to make their dreams real. They don't even feel as if they're working. Entrepreneurs are doing something they find interesting, something they love and find "fun." Sir Noel Coward said, "Work is more fun than fun." Entrepreneurs agree with Sir Noel.

Harold Geneen's fame as an extremely capable manager is exceeded, perhaps, only by his reputation as someone who works long and hard. He kept stacks of large briefcases in his office—a dozen or more at all times—each filled with a different project for him to take with him for whenever there might be a spare moment, to ensure that he'd always have plenty of work to do.

Geneen is 82 now and still works long, hard hours. When I asked him if he was a workaholic, he laughed. He doesn't think he works at all. To him it's fun. Work is his hobby. His passion, though, is not the work, but the dream. The work is merely the process to convert his dreams to reality. He doesn't lug around those briefcases to look busy or to fill his time. He uses the briefcases and their contents as his tool kit to build his dreams.

Entrepreneurs may work hard, but they are not workaholics. The entrepreneurs' work ethic is a "dream ethic," to do whatever is necessary to convert their dream to a reality.

Profile

Sherren Leigh and the "Part-Time" Entrepreneur

Usually, entrepreneurs exert their confidence to pursue their dreams, whereas workaholics' lack of confidence fuels their neuroses. Sometimes, though, individuals possess both sets of traits.

Sherren Leigh struck gold with conventions for women managers. Sherren's pioneering effort in Chicago drew 17,000 women—not the 3000 to 4000 she had expected, so she was soon offering conventions in seven cities a year. Once, while promoting a Houston convention, she noticed that ads placed in a local women's newspaper drew more responses than either of the city's major dailies, even though it was a less polished production. The paper succeeded because it reached an otherwise untapped market.

So Sherren founded *Today's Chicago Woman* and continued to run the convention businesses as well. In reality, she only had time for one, the convention business, and because it was the comfortable old shoe, it got the attention. In time, her chores became wearing. Frequent stays in her convention cities convinced her the food was getting worse and worse. "I can't look at iceberg lettuce without snarling at it," she says. She was working 80-hour weeks, clearly becoming a drudge if not a workaholic, and her new newspaper was suffering benign neglect and losing large sums of money.

Her accountant set her straight. He said, "You've got to look at this [*Today's Chicago Woman*] as a separate profit center. You are losing close to $500,000 a year." The conventions had been doing well enough that she easily covered the shortfall at the newspaper.

But her accountant pressed the issue. He said, "Would you give that money to charity?" Sherren said, "No. I don't have that kind of money to give to charity."

"Then how can you give it to a project that you have no interest in? Because you are not giving the newspaper any of your attention." She knew he was right.

But it took personal tragedy to change her ways. After watching in agony for years as two people close to her deteriorated and then died, she resolved that life was more important than money. "What is important are relationships with people; taking care of yourself. It is getting out on a beautiful day and being able to walk along the beach before it gets dark. You can have more money than you will ever spend, if you put money first and life second." She was no longer willing to do that. Sherren was sick of riding the "B" city circuit, as she refers to the second-tier cities that made up her convention beat. Sherren, who had a degree in journalism, began focusing attention on the newspaper and downscaling the convention side of her business.

Sherren adjusted her dreams to fit her willing effort and, in so doing, became more productive: "In focusing our attention on the newspaper and building it into a profitable entity, there was more of a quality to my life, because I enjoy publishing a paper more than I enjoy visiting towns like Pittsburgh and Minneapolis and St. Louis." Sherren also has become a part-time entrepreneur. She has cut her work week in half—to 40 hours from 80. She says that if you want to excel in business, you work hard and work smart: "As long as you are going to be in the work force from 9 to 5, if you do your best, you'll shine and you will come through at the top." Those are an intense 40 hours, she admits, and her employees confirm this. But 40 hours are all it takes.

If you work 80 hours a week because you love your work, you may be a workaholic. If, instead, you work that hard because that's what it takes to make your dream real, then you're probably an entrepreneur. If 80 hours is just too much, it doesn't matter whether you adjust your dream as Sherren did or simply increase your efficiency. Either way, your effort should be focused to accomplish your dream.

Sherren Leigh's Secret Weapon

Entrepreneurs must have either self-confidence or self-esteem. Some, like Sherren Leigh, have both. "I have a lot of confidence in myself because, I don't like to use a cliché but for lack of better words, you are your own event. Early on, I realized that Mr. Right was not going to make my life great, because there is no such thing....You create your own area in life, an arena. I am happy with what I have done. I have good self-esteem because I like myself."

Point of Information

Long Hours Do Not a Workaholic Make

By any test, Microsoft's septibillionaire, Bill Gates, 37, cofounder of the company that dominates the software for desktop computing, works very hard. He tells biographers he has slowed his work schedule to 72 hours a week. "I mean, I assume you don't count reading business magazines, the *Journal*, or the *Economist*."

And like so many other hard workers, he is driven not by overconfidence but by insecurity. In his case, he fears rivals are gaining and can turn victory into defeat. So apart from occasional breaks to read and sleep—at times under an office table—Gates is rarely off the job and out racing the Porches and Jaguars he loves to drive.

There are other entrepreneurs who work equally hard. Many of them feel there is a whip behind them that drives them on. (Managers see a whip in front.) Even so, some highly successful entrepreneurs hold their hours in check. Those entrepreneurs know that relaxation and fun should be features of every successful life. Some entrepreneurs are as driven as Bill Gates and simply cannot quit. When Bill Gates recently announced his engagement to marry a midlevel executive at Microsoft, his competitors were ecstatic, anticipating a reduction in his competitive efforts. Time will tell.

Pride Can Shape Your Work Ethic

While outsiders, such as parents, can instill a work ethic, ultimately your work ethic is internal. If you want to be an entrepreneur, then you must look for your work ethic deep inside yourself. What causes you to work hard—to drive, compete, and strive to beat—is a feeling, a caring about how well you do. That feeling is pride.

Pat Ryan is the founder of Aon, one of the largest insurance companies as a result of his acquisition of W. Clement Stone's Combined Insurance. Ryan talked about pride in two veins. According to Ryan, public pride, often referred to as ego, must be kept under control. Otherwise, it moves ahead of liquor, sex, and gambling as the major cause of business downfall. Private pride, however, is what Pat Ryan believes motivates him. Ryan long ago decided to "succeed unusually." To do less would imply he was capable of less, and Pat Ryan's pride would not tolerate that. As a result, Pat's pride takes over, gives him "a big kick," and makes him "dig deep" to "succeed unusually."

In going back and rereading the transcripts of many of the interviews that led to this book, I found pride to be one of the most consistently expressed concepts. Debbi Fields put it most succinctly; her slogan is: "Good enough never is." Edson de Castro, the founder of Data General, left Digital Equipment Corporation (DEC) and formed Data General because the bureaucracy at DEC precluded his attaining the level of excellence consistent with his standards for pride. Eileen Ford thought the two model agencies in business when she started were terrible (the principal of one wound up in jail), so they couldn't be her employers. They clearly didn't meet her standards and couldn't offer her pride in her work.

While many entrepreneurs measure themselves against their own standards, some allow others to do the measuring. Richie

Melman and Jovan Trboyevic, the consummate restauranteurs, take little solace in their great track records but consider their patrons to be the critics who judge their decor, theme, ambience, menu, food, presentation, and service. Richie and Jovan say their patrons' faces tell them when they can be proud of what they have done. It's OK for the measuring to be done by someone else because Richie and Jovan derive their pride from empowering their customers to measure them.

The standard that most entrepreneurs set for themselves is to be among the best at what they do. Some, like Jovan Trboyevic, who recently sold his third highly successful restaurant, seek to outdo their own track records. He told me, "This is my cause. I am like a one-woman man. I am a one-restaurant man. I compete against the previous one and want this to be the best." Most entrepreneurs want to be the best they can be.

Therefore, if you want to be an entrepreneur, adopt standards that relate to your being the best—the best there is, the best you can be, or the best you have been—at the process of making your dream real. Setting the standards makes them yours, your path to your way. To own the path, you must use it. To be proud, you must not only set your own standards but also do unusual things to achieve them.

Profile

Elmer Stokes*: Secret Agent in a Business Suit (Pride Goeth before a Push Broom)

Elmer Stokes looked like any other member of the establishment before and after he became an entrepreneur. His uniform was correct, from his carefully pressed suit and carefully tied tie down to the Cross pen in his breast pocket, his weapon in life.

One day not long after Elmer had gone into business for himself, I got a suspicious call from his accountant. The accountant said, "There is something funny going on out there. I read the lease and it doesn't show a clause for a clean up service. Is there any?"

I said, "I have no idea." We did the lease, but I didn't handle it personally. So I called one of our real estate lawyers who did. He said, Elmer Stokes had specifically negotiated cleaning service out of the lease and "got himself a reduction in rent."

My client's accountant wasn't satisfied. He said Stokes hadn't given him any bills from a clean up service. I said, "Well, why don't you ask the client about it?"

As it turns out, every night after all the employees left, Elmer would take off his jacket, roll up his shirt sleeves, put on a smock, and empty all the waste baskets.

He gathered all the trash and threw it into the dumpster out back. He swept the floor and washed it. He washed down anything else that needed it, too. He did it all, staying until midnight, tackling whatever it took to put the place in order. The plain fact was he couldn't afford to hire a janitorial service. When the accountant confronted the entrepreneur, he confessed that he was doing the nightly clean-up. His public pride made him wear a suit and tie to work. His private pride wasn't bruised when he did his own cleaning. That's what it took to realize his dream.

Six Steps to Structuring Your Dream

Use the Law of Sympathetic Resonance

In the 1600s, Christian Huygens invented the pendulum clock. He displayed his clocks on the walls of a room, where each pendulum swung independently. Huygens discovered that, after awhile, all the pendula began to swing in precise, synchronized rhythm. He theorized that the clocks' sound waves entered the walls, which responded with their own vibrations, thereby bringing the clocks into a single rhythm. Huygens' theory is now a well accepted law of physics, known as "sympathetic resonance."

As you begin to dream, your dream's rhythm will be affected just like the response of the walls to all the other sound waves in the room. So do your dreaming in the company of "clocks" whose rhythm you want to emulate.

As a child, when you wanted to do or buy a certain thing, you knew which parent to ask because that parent would be more supportive of your goal than the other. As a student, you knew which teacher to approach with your ideas or questions. Even now, you know which supervisor, boss, or colleague will create the vibrations most harmonious to your own.

If you are thinking about starting or acquiring your own business, hang around people who have been or are entrepreneurs. Don't try to work amidst the din of naysayers. They send out vibrations of "can't do" and "can't be done" which are so strong that, if you are hanging around them, they, like the walls behind the clocks, will cause you to swing in sync with them. And that will deter you from your dream.

The vibrations of such naysayers are predictable. For years, I have used an expression to describe the reactions of professionals who were not versed in an innovative legal, tax, or financial technique proposed by me or my firm. The expression is, "If you're not up on it, you've got to be down on it."

You must surround yourself with people who are "up on it"— who understand your need to pursue an entrepreneurial dream.

Do Your Homework

To compensate for a low metabolism and a healthy appetite, I work out every day by riding 15 miles on a stationary bike. I joke that, on weekends, I do a civilized triathalon, by swimming in my pool, riding an exercycle, and taking a nap. When I travel, I try to stay at hotels that will bring an exercycle to my room. People I deal with learned of this eccentricity, so it was no surprise when an Israeli patent lawyer I was dealing with asked me to meet with his client who had invented a portable exercycle that could fit in a briefcase.

This was intriguing. I could see the market potential and certainly I could personally appreciate the product. I could visualize ads in the airline magazines and the product in airport concession stores. Everything seemed great, and I was ready to undertake this business opportunity for a particular client. But first I knew some homework was required. In order to undertake the marketing and manufacturing tool-up expenses, my client would require protection from competition, lest he pay to develop a product line for others.

I negotiated a deal where my client would undertake a patent search, in return for an option to buy the inventor's rights on a royalty basis. The patent search revealed patents on dozens of portable exercycles; there was no way to obtain the requisite protection. My initial dream was of a reality that I thought didn't exist, I really was dreaming about a reality that was and was and was. My homework saved me from a potential disaster.

Select What You Care About

Richie Melman said, "Do what you know and love." Unfortunately, many would-be entrepreneurs are frustrated doing what they know, and others have never experienced a business they could love.

You may hate your job simply because it is a job. You very well might love the business you're in, if you could find a better boss and stay in the same business. Be sure which part you hate. If you hate the business, then you certainly shouldn't go into it on your own. If all you hate is working for someone else, then do what it takes to change that but stick with the business you know.

You needn't have experience in the business you could love in order to be successful in it. Diane Freis, who built and owns an international clothing business, knew nothing about clothes designing and manufacturing. She was a sculptress who, needing to make ends meet, designed and sewed some jackets for a Rodeo Drive boutique. When the jackets were gobbled up by Diana Ross, Elke Sommers, and Joni Mitchell, Diane entered the fashion business.

Care About What You Select

We are not discussing run-of-the-mill dreams. We are talking about your big-time dream, which will lift you out of the depths of working for someone else and elevate you to the heights of entrepreneurship.

I have met and known entrepreneurs whose dreams were so vital and critical to them that they ignored their children, sacrificed their friends, disregarded their spouses, and neglected the basics of human existence—food, health care, sleep, recreation, and sex. Why? Because, in entrepreneurship, they found a passion that superseded any other passions in their lives. Entrepreneurship can become psychologically addictive and lends itself, if unchecked, to extremism.

Your passion for entrepreneurship must know some moderation. Human beings must leave time and space for a variety of human pursuits. You can be passionate with each of your pursuits, but mere diversification brings moderation. When you are an entrepreneur, you will be passionate about your dream, but you can also care very much about the other aspects of your life.

Don't Bite Off More Than You Can Chew

Kids always fill their plates with more goodies than they can possibly eat, and parents always tell them that their eyes are bigger than their stomachs. As you select and fashion your entrepreneurial dream, make sure your eyes aren't too big for your stomach.

When Thurman Rodgers left American Microsystems, where his project had failed, he tried to raise $30 million from the venture capital community to start his own business. He was unsuccessful because he had no track record and didn't understand venture financing. Instead, he had to go to work for another boss, Advance Micro Devices. Attempting to start his own business, at that time, was biting off more than he could chew.

Dream as big an entrepreneurial dream as you like, but when you are ready to implement it, be sensible and size your dream to your life. It may be difficult to do, especially the first time you try. Don't let that stop you. You know you must try, even if you might fail. But nothing says you have to be foolish and increase your likelihood of failure, so take the time to assess yourself and gauge your dreams accordingly.

Bill Farley is known as an aggressive risk taker. His acquisition of West Point-Pepperill was highly leveraged through Mike Milken's junk bonds. The likelihood of Farley's success or failure was the subject of debate for years before the axe of Chapter VII (bankruptcy) finally fell. When I asked Farley how he decided whether to do a particular deal, he referred to the phrase "rational optimism," which he described as follows: "When I try to buy West Point-Pepperill, I know there's a good probability of my doing it. I didn't try to buy General Motors. There is a rationality to what I am doing; it is within a framework that I can deal with."

Times change and the ability to judge deals in their proper time frame can be difficult, so we may never know if Farley's deal was intelligently optimistic or just optimistic, and it really doesn't matter. The concept of rational optimism is sound. Stretching optimistically is rational too, and that's what entrepreneurial dreaming is about. But be sensible about how you stretch. That's what being an entrepreneur is all about.

Start Early and Often and Be Patient

"Start early and be patient" is not the same as "Hurry up and wait." There is no waiting involved here. Instead, I want you to follow the old adage in Chicago elections: "Vote early and vote often." You must begin the process now and start over each and every day.

Although you will be making progress, having to start over each day will make you feel as though you are standing still. That is why you will need patience. Don't feel frustrated. Try to see your progress, even though it is less than obvious. Even if your progress is invisible, have faith—be patient—it is happening. After all, if you can see reality that doesn't exist, you should be able to believe in progress you can't see.

10

Entrepreneurs Are Mavericks Who Start Stampedes

To consider oneself different from ordinary men
is wrong, but it is right to hope that one will
not remain like ordinary men.

YOSHIDA SHORIN ZENSHU

Dan Tolkowsky has successfully capitalized entrepreneurs' ventures for over three decades. In selecting recipients of his backing, he considers the customary factors—integrity, business sense, leadership, etc.—but he told me he also seeks and backs "mavericks":

> I've never minded odd people, you know, the mavericks, the unusual guys. I've always looked for people who are unusual in that sense. It is extremely easy to say, "I'm looking for people who are my kind." Well, that's bullshit. You need people who are good in their own way. They may be odd or unusual; chances are they are. If they weren't they probably wouldn't become entrepreneurs.

What does it take to be enough of a maverick to attract the backing of venture capitalists without being strange enough to

105

scare them off? When you march to a different drummer, how do you know whether you are creative or so far off the beaten path as to be bizarre? When does unconventional behavior or thought prove valuable and when is it detrimental? Doing different things or doing things differently is not mutually exclusive with doing business. The test is not so much how you behave but how your behavior impacts your business life.

Some entrepreneurs are artists or inventors. There is a tendency to think of all entrepreneurs as artists or inventors, perhaps because some of the most famous ones were. George Eastman, Edwin Land, Stephen Jobs, Calvin Klein, and Walt Disney, all artists and inventors, are among the world's best-known entrepreneurs.

Yet, artists and inventors make up only a small part of the entrepreneurial community. So, it is important to separate the art of invention from the art of business.

The traditional images of artists and inventors contrast strikingly with those of business people. The Bohemian artist and the absent-minded, hermitlike inventor have perceptions that vary so much that we sometimes wonder whether they merely see the world differently or actually live in different worlds. Yet, that different perception is their basic talent. How they control, tolerate, and shape that talent determines whether they also can succeed as entrepreneurs.

Efi Arazi, the founder of Scitex, is both inventor and entrepreneur but understands the difference. He cautions a wannabe entrepreneur who begins as a technologist "to check whether he is not just an accomplished nerd." You know what a "nerd" is, don't you? He's the high school classmate you barely knew who wore a plastic pocket protector and who recently sold his computer company for $50 million. Some nerd, huh?

Diane Freis, a sculptress by training, designed some jackets to make ends meet. The jackets were a surprise hit in a Rodeo Drive store, leading Diane to start a clothing business which has become an international company. Diane views entrepreneurs as "creative entities" and feels that being an entrepreneur has served her well by satisfying her desire for "more and more artistic expression."

Gordon Segal was willing to form a business, even though he

was "not as interested in the business as in the art of business." Gordon "wanted to be off-the-wall different." He succeeded, and his Crate & Barrel stores continue to set trends.

Bernard Goldhirsh worked for Ed Land after MIT and was on his way to being an inventor. His artistic flair led him to his first business; he founded *Sail Magazine,* which related to his love, sailing. His own shortcoming in starting that business showed him a need for a magazine to guide entrepreneurs and small business people, so he "invented" *Inc.*

The land of entrepreneurship is indeed a fertile field for inventors and artists who can combine what Diane Freis calls "the financial backdrop" with "the pursuit of artistic expressions." The fields are equally fertile, too, for those who are neither artists nor inventors.

Some people are artistic and inventive but are not artists or inventors. If they were, their unique approach might seem normal. In the business world, they often seem odd. Phil Romano, the entrepreneur who founded Fuddruckers and Romano's Macaroni Grill, uses restaurants as his palette. He says "entrepreneurs are very different" because, unlike most people, who neither need nor desire a change from the status quo, entrepreneurs "can't cope with the way things are and are willing to take a different approach."

On the one hand, artists are supposed to push the envelope, do the unexpected; the businessperson, on the other hand, who takes a moderately different approach may seem to be outrageous. These conventions made it more difficult for businesspeople to get away with unique behavior. First of all, doing so makes one a target. As the Pittsburgh industrialist Henry Hillman said, "only the whale who spouts gets harpooned." Second, our society emits so many contradictory—and counterproductive—messages. Do you still hear your parents asking why you can't be like all the other kids? It's not easy to realize that being different can be positive, especially after years of hearing other messages. Who emulates a maverick when the common role model is so highly praised? An entrepreneur, that's who.

Some entrepreneurs have novel personal styles that shape and enhance their businesses. Their uniqueness often generates great publicity. Innumerable articles have been written—some even accurately—about the dress and behavior of Sam Zell, Ben Cohen, and Hugh Hefner. All favor casual attire and have highly individualistic personalities. Their unique styles convinced them that they could not work for someone else. That's why the talented and successful venture capitalist Roe Stamps refers to entrepreneurs as "unemployable." They must become entrepreneurs.

Sam Zell could easily afford expensive designer suits and a chauffeur-driven limousine. Instead, when Zell goes to work, he dons his blue jeans, hops on his motorcycle, and chauffeurs himself to his office. Zell has been able to raise billions recently from investors who believe in his contrarian theory of buying when everyone is selling. Others may share Zell's theories, but Zell uses his image of being successfully different to attract the capital that lets him profit from being different over and over again.

Ben Cohen's difference is not limited to his casual attire and appearances. He believes in and supports environmental causes, something he did before it was fashionable. Part of the profits from certain Ben and Jerry's products is contributed to those causes. He and his partner, Jerry Greenfield, also established compensation ratios, where their company's highest-paid executives cannot make more than five times the compensation of the lowest-paid employee. Their program has created excellent employee morale and public relations. Their policies also help their business. It seems that the people who buy Ben and Jerry's ice cream feel proud that their purchase does good things. With motives as pure as his ingredients, Ben has found a way to convert his differences to assets.

Today, Hugh Hefner probably seems like any other man in his sixties with a young wife and toddler. However, when he started *Playboy*, his "decadent" lifestyle contrasted violently with society's norms. Not many men were able to spend all day in pajamas, with pipe and Pepsi, surrounded by a bevy of voluptuous women who shared his "Playboy philosophy." Here, too, consumers related to what the entrepreneur did, even if they couldn't do it themselves. Sure, men bought the magazine to see the pictures, but they also bought the symbols of the lifestyle—

clubs, resorts, matches, ashtrays, clothing—as if those items could provide Hef's lifestyle. Some people would have been embarrassed to publicize such a lifestyle. Hefner used it to strengthen his product.

Reality Artists

Another group of entrepreneurs, no less different in their business endeavors, are pillars of the community. Their personal lives and appearances reflect the community's norms and standards. Unlike Cohen, Zell, and Hefner, these entrepreneurs don't look or dress differently. They come to business from a business background. They are as much a maverick as the artists and inventors but differ in other ways. Their approach is all business. Their canvasses are financial statements and contracts. They are steeped in reality.

Fred Smith, the founder of Federal Express, broke two important rules. First, he defied conventional wisdom, which many people believed was the law, that only the U.S. Postal Service could deliver the mail. Second, he broke a law of geometry—that the shortest distance between two points is a straight line—when he routed all packages through Memphis.

Gary Rosenberg, who founded UDC Homes, devised new techniques for financing his company's acquisition of land, development of properties, and construction of fine homes. He did all that in ways that "had never been done," "couldn't be done," and that "anyone else could copy." But, he did them, successfully.

Fred Smith recalled reading about Hannibal, who shocked the world by coming over the Alps on elephants. Gary Rosenberg read about Albert Einstein and was awed by Einstein's willingness to think new thoughts and contradict "laws of science." But they both learned from books the value of being different and breaking rules, and each applied the principle, positively and constructively.

Being different can yield dividends, but you may pay a price. The key is how you handle being different. You may look at reality from another perspective, as Smith and Rosenberg learned to do, or change your lifestyle so your differences improve your business, as Zell, Cohen, and Hefner did. If you are in the business of art, where you see the unreal and portray it with real images, remember that you are also involved in the art of business, where—no matter how different you are, how many rules you break, or how art-oriented your product or services—you always must see reality.

Be Comfortable Being Different

Jim Henson's Kermit the Frog identified the problem for most of us when he said: "It isn't easy being green." It takes guts and confidence to be different; it takes style to make being a maverick an asset rather than a liability. Guts, confidence, and style are the prerequisites to being comfortable with being different, and that's the same at every level of economic or social status.

Certain entrepreneurs get comfortable being different because of their relationship with their parents. For years, Larry Levy sought approval from his father, the dominant personality in his family and a highly successful promoter of stars such as Fats Domino, Little Richard, Chuck Berry, Bobby Darin, Paul Anka, Steve Lawrence and Eydie Gorme, and Joan Baez. Larry's father represented artists and respected their ability to be different. Larry believed his father wanted him to emulate that attribute. Larry realized early that "I only got approval when I did something good and different. What he liked was that I did something that other kids didn't do." Even when he founded The Levy Restaurants, which owns or operates 35 restaurants and runs Specialty Concessions, serving McCormick Place, Navy Pier, Wrigley Field, White Sox Park, Ravinia Park, Goodman Theater, Arlington Race Track, and Disney World, he was doing it to please his father. After his father died, Larry began to work for his own approval but continued to value and be comfortable doing what others don't or can't do.

Some entrepreneurs use the "ostrich theory." They blind themselves to their unique characteristics. A perfect example may be Dennis Keller, the president of the DeVry schools. Dennis grew up in Hinsdale, a Chicago suburb where TV shows like "Father Knows Best" and "Ozzie and Harriet" could have been filmed, indeed, where they could have been lived. People in Hinsdale, like many other people, prefer to think of themselves as "much like all the other folks in Hinsdale."

Dennis told me that he was a run-of-the-mill kid in Hinsdale and had never done anything other than what was expected of a Hinsdale kid. Later in the interview, I learned that the Keller basement had been turned into an aviary by young Dennis, who started a business breeding and selling birds. Somehow, I doubt that all the other Hinsdale basements had scores of birds flying around.

Dennis did not consider himself different, despite his bird business (the only one in Hinsdale) and his Princeton Pizza business (the only one at Princeton University where very few students had jobs, let alone businesses that out-earned the professors). While Dennis had been groomed in the Hinsdale tradition—of thinking he was "much like all the other folks in Hinsdale"—deep down, Dennis knew he was very different from the other folks. He was comfortable being different, even though he "hid" the difference in the basement, as well as in the recesses of his mind.

That comfort with being different served Dennis well. When he left his job at Bell & Howell, he founded the Keller School of Management, which became the only privately owned school awarding MBA degrees and which later acquired DeVry, the largest school in the United States. Eventually DeVry sold its stock to the public, becoming the first such school to do so. Dennis is so comfortable being different that he doesn't even realize how different he is.

Another example of an entrepreneur who denied being different was Sybil Ferguson, the founder of Diet Centers. Unlike Keller, whose denial was based on his community's standards, Sybil's denial was her own defense mechanism to avoid being hurt. Long before she followed her doctor's advice to charge those she was helping lose weight, Sybil Ferguson had tried desperately and in vain to help herself, using the time-honored approach of counting calories. Of course, skipping nutritional food but having a 500-calorie candy bar to stay under 1000 calories per day didn't work. Eventually, Sybil realized that, went to the library to do some research, and developed the weight loss plan, based on nutrition and exercise, that worked first on Sybil, then on her doctor's patients, and, ultimately, on thousands of Diet Centers' customers.

When I suggested to Sybil that she was a bit of a rule breaker because she broke with the custom of calorie counting, she objected. Sybil, who is very active in her church and community, seemed insulted that I insinuated that she was a rule breaker. She objected, "I developed a program based on sound tradition, so it's not breaking rules. It's breaking with what people accepted."

Sybil's point is that you must look beyond what appears to be. Even if a particular course of action is customary, such as counting calories to lose weight, it may be a relatively recent custom. The real rule may be so far back that it has been forgotten. So, forsaking calorie counting and reverting to that older format was not breaking a rule but going back to a more basic rule.

Sybil's point is interesting, but I don't buy it. I think her background and lifestyle caused her to reject what I considered a compliment—that she is willing to break the right rules to make things better—when, in fact, she is actually quite comfortable with being different and breaking rules.

To understand Sybil's defensiveness, you must know something about her background. While in third grade, Sybil fell and broke her two front teeth, which turned black. Her schoolmates taunted her—even tying her to a tree. They would touch her, then touch other kids, saying "Now, you've got Sybil on you." As a result, for years, Sybil could not speak in front of a group of people. Fairly recently, Sybil regained her ability to speak in public. You might think she was spurred on by the constant image of her competitor, Jenny Craig, on TV commercials. Actually, her feeling of responsibility to make her business a success made her take lessons and overcome her disability. Now, she is her company's spokesperson.

It isn't easy being green. Often, you become the spouting whale, the target of schoolmates' or neighbors' harpoons or recall the fragile times in your life. Some peoples' motivations for being different may seem strange. It doesn't matter how you happen to learn that it's OK to be different, who encourages you or whom you do it for, so long as you learn to be comfortable being different. If you must hide your differences, as Dennis did, in order to be comfortable, that's all right. If, like Sybil, you are forced to confront being different, then use the lessons to gain strength and comfort about being different. Just being an entrepreneur will make you different, and you must be comfortable with that.

Profile

Gary Greenberg: The Unemployable

Small boys often defy authority and come to grief. Gary Greenberg did that constantly. But, like some other renegades, he was destined to be an entrepreneur.

Gary and his buddies prowled Chicago's north side looking for trouble and quite naturally found it. "We probably didn't do anything any different than anybody else did—but we got caught." Far too often, it seems. Gary's last trip to the police station was at age 14. This time a female police officer got through to him. Much tougher than most of the male officers, she stared at Gary without emotion and said, "Greenberg, you have been here so often in the last couple of years, I am telling you the next time you are in here, you are not leaving." Says Gary, "That had been said to me many times before, but the way she said it and the way she looked at me, that stuck. Fortunately, I was never back there again."

Gary was certainly sarcastic. "I had a mouth. When I felt that there was something that was right, I wasn't afraid to tell a teacher or principal that I was right and they were wrong. They didn't like that. That was up against authority."

Gary continued his studies at the University of Oklahoma and graduated in 1969. Being very personable and a good salesperson, Gary was offered so many jobs that he didn't know which to take. Finally he accepted a position with a small food broker for $125 a week. He took the job because the boss agreed to train him in every aspect of the business. Gary went through the program and befriended Shel Stillman, a coworker who, at age 28, was six years older. Shel was one of the best salespeople in the company. In a telling episode, the star salesperson had decided to ask the boss for a small raise on a salary Gary thought ridiculous in view of the man's performance. Gary told his friend that modest though the raise request was, the boss was a cheapskate who would try to reduce the request by 10 percent. The older man was astonished when the scenario played out exactly as Gary had predicted it would. They left together. It was the beginning of a rapport and a partnership that would last for many years.

Gary Greenberg's Secret Weapon: Learn by Doing

Gary Greenberg's partner was at an airlines seminar at Cornell University in 1971. The airlines complained that there was no specialized distribution system for serving millions of meals every year. The problem was to get perishable product from the producer and into the flight kitchens in cities all around the United States.

Gary's partner raced home to convince Gary this was a natural. Gary's partner was an experienced food broker, but they naturally made lots of mistakes. According to Gary, "I would say that Shelly and I always said that we are going to make some mistakes. We are going to stub our toe, we are going to learn, we are going to lose some money. There is not too much we are going to be able to do about it."

The business grew to $7 million, to $10 million, to $30 million, and then to $50 million. Says Gary, "We'd say, 'We're not geniuses. What experience do we have running a $50 million company? None. Zero.' We weren't schooled. We didn't have MBAs. We didn't go to the managerial programs. We were learning by baptism. So we make mistakes." But they didn't focus on the money lost in making mistakes. They focused instead on what they could learn from their business mistakes.

Gary Greenberg cofounded a business that brokered food to the airlines. The business grew so big that it was acquired by Kraft. Gary had to confront being different. He went his own way for he loathes authority so much that he simply couldn't wear the straightjacket of employment. But Kraft couldn't run the business as well and so sold it back to Gary and his partner.

Doing What Comes Naturally

By the time most of us learn about famous entrepreneurs, they are successful and accomplished. By then, they seem to have adapted naturally to all that came their way. The truth is more complex. The entrepreneurs' natural adaptation to the ultimate challenges were possible because of the strength these people gained dealing with earlier difficulties. The entrepreneurs were able to make an asset out of being different because they never let their earlier differences become a liability.

Joe Sullivan, the turnaround expert at Swift/Esmark, fired his boss when he was close to 50 and, with funding from Sam Zell, entered the food and agriculture products businesses in the early 1980s, when everyone had written off those industries. One of his companies, Vigaro, recently went public, and the others seem to be doing well. Why was Joe so comfortable hoeing such a different row?

Remember how Joe Sullivan learned what it meant to be different when he grew up in the Brighton district of Boston. As an Irish Catholic in a Brahmin town, Joe accepted the fact of being different but searched for ways to make the difference work for him. In the Army, the ultimate bastion of conformity, while others were satisfied being "at ease," Joe started two businesses. Soon his battalion commander named him "Lieutenant Bilko," after the Phil Silvers TV character Sgt. Bilko, who embodied all the good and bad elements of entrepreneurship. After the Army, Joe's childhood need to fit in with the "in group" probably led him to Swift—as old-line a company as you can find. Even at staid Swift/Esmark, Joe pushed to bend the company's rules and red tape whenever he thought doing so would benefit the company. He continued seeking ways to make an asset out of being different. By the time he left Swift, he was ready for the likes of Sam Zell and his contrarian approach to business.

Raymond Hung was born and raised in Hong Kong but was fortunate to be sent to college in the United States. After receiving his undergraduate degree in engineering from the University of Illinois and his MBA from the University of Chicago, he could have had his pick of jobs with prime American companies. That opportunity is what motivates many young people to emigrate to the United States. Raymond is not like most people. Instead, to the shock and chagrin of his classmates, Raymond initially went to work for a small Hong Kong company and made far less money than his classmates. A few years later, he founded Applied International Holdings, Ltd., a successful consumer products company whose securities are now traded over the Hong Kong exchange.

Had he remained in the United States, Raymond would have been different. Even though Hong Kong was his birthplace, his American education made him different there too. Raymond realized that, in America, his difference might prove disadvantageous, while in Hong Kong, his unique education could work to his benefit. Raymond found a way to combine the strength of uniqueness with the comfort of familiar surroundings.

The Natural Site

It's natural for a location or business to seem unnatural if it has never been done before. Frequently, however, entrepreneurs feel natural about a location being so different.

When Marilyn Miglin noticed that models and entertainers travelled to New York to buy the makeup that was unavailable elsewhere, she decided to open a store in Chicago that would carry those products. That was a bold endeavor; after all there must have been a good reason that no one else opened such a store outside of New York. Her Chicago store prospered, and now her products include Pheromone and Destiny perfumes, which are sold nationwide.

Marilyn Miglin learned what it meant to be different when she was nine and her father died. All her classmates had both parents, and she felt very different. In fact, Marilyn told me, when her class sang the line in "America," that goes "...land where our fathers died," she was certain that everyone in class was staring at her. If she was going to be stared at for being different, she decided to make it a positive event. Marilyn worked very hard at her ballet lessons and became quite good. Standing out from the crowd became a goal, not an ordeal. She became a "Chez Paree Adorable," as the dancers at that famous nightclub were known, and later was one of the dancers in Jimmy

Durante's troupe. To this day, Marilyn stands out in a crowd, both because she continues to look like an "Adorable" some 30 years after retiring and because of her unique and successful approach to her business.

It wasn't easy, but Marilyn had learned at nine to accept and cope with her biggest difference, so her differences later on seemed natural. After that first step, it was easy for Marilyn to go into a different business and do it so differently. After all, to Marilyn, being different had long ago become part of her routine.

It's not necessary to share the unique backgrounds of any of these entrepreneurs. Your childhood had its own elements of being different; we all had them. The secret is recognizing and using your own differences—whether good or bad—to achieve a positive result. You must perceive the glass containing your differences, no matter what their flavor, as half-full, not half-empty.

Joe Sullivan could have felt like an oppressed minority and spent all his energy assimilating and avoiding being different. And Marilyn Miglin could have continued in the chorus line of show business, instead of opening a new place where her new boss was the primo ballerina.

The lesson for Joe and Marilyn could have been: "I've carried enough burdens in life, now I don't have to." Instead, they said, "My burdens developed a strength which I can use to my advantage." That's what you must do. And because the relevant background is your own background, using it to your benefit will give you a natural advantage, even if it doesn't feel natural at first.

Divergent-Path Syndrome

You possess many of the traits you need to become an entrepreneur, but they are hidden from your view because of what I call the "divergent-path syndrome." Most of us make very important vocational decisions in our late teens or early twenties. We *tend* to select a particular path—business, education, technological, public service, social welfare—that we plan to follow all our lives. The paths are not parallel but resemble a bicycle's spokes, starting close together but separating more as you get further from the hub. As we get older, the separation between our path and the other paths increases, and the other paths seem more difficult. The thought of jumping over the widening gap to one of those paths becomes frightening.

Your path may have taken you so far in another direction that you can't see your way clear to jumping to the entrepreneurs' paths. The way they march on their path may seem anything but natural to you. Here are a few pointers that may help you.

1. *Your teachers chose a different path.* With rare exception, teachers choose the academic, not the entrepreneurial, path. That is why, as Ned Heizer pointed out, they are prone to teach risk avoidance. Good teachers are necessary and invaluable; they deserve no less respect—perhaps they deserve more— for having chosen their path. However, it is important that you recognize what path they are on before you accept their teachings. Their influence on path selection tends to be subtle. They don't say, "Take this path rather than the entrepreneurial path." Instead, they say, "On this multiple choice exam, you will be penalized for wrong answers." Even in business schools, teachers say, "In this case study, how would you solve the company's problems without jeopardizing its steady income stream?" You might disagree and decide that a brief interruption in income is justified if the result is a substantive correction in the underlying business. I suggest that you always seek both answers. Give the teacher the expected answer, and you decide which you would use in real life.

2. *Your original choice may not be your best choice.* At the original hub, there were two factors—your ability and your choice. The fact that you chose one path doesn't mean that you weren't able to choose a different path. It is possible that you would have been better at travelling that other path.

3. *You do get a second chance.* The original hub isn't your only hub. The point you are at now can be a new hub with new choices and paths.

4. *Not only wine improves with age.* Your capabilities now may be very different than those you had at the original hub.

Therefore, new paths may be open to you and new choices may be appropriate.

You may be suffering from the divergent-path syndrome, but your cure can be at hand. Step back, consider what influenced your path, as well as how you and the world have changed. Then, prepare to start over.

From Rogues to Riches

Al Capone was an entrepreneur, but he's never referred to that way. Just how far can one go before the title "entrepreneur" is replaced with "gangster"? When does a "pro" become a "con"?

Professor Mort Kamien, who holds the Heizer Chair in Entrepreneurship at Kellogg, asked me how I was going to deal with the ghetto kids who push drugs. Although those kids are entrepreneurs, I intend to limit this book to legitimate enterprise. Yet, so many entrepreneurs related childhood rebellions, which in some cases involved minor law breaking, that I had to treat the phenomenon.

I do not propose or condone breaking any laws, but I did notice that many entrepreneurs felt comfortable about having broken certain laws. Almost without exception, entrepreneurs who break such laws stay on the safe side of an all-important line. Knowing the location of that narrow line is important; it may be a talent or may be luck. The line, however, is very narrow and can be deceptive.

In many cities during the 1950s, it was illegal to sell *Playboy*. One such city was Highland Park, Illinois, the Chicago suburb where Sam Zell grew up. Sam took the elevated train after school to attend religious school in Chicago. He discovered that *Playboy* was sold at the Chicago "el" newsstand, so he bought several copies each day to sell to students at Highland Park High School. Jerry Reinsdorf, the successful real estate entrepreneur who now owns the Chicago Bulls and Chicago White Sox, grew up in Brooklyn. Although his parents weren't particularly well off, Jerry didn't have to work while going to grammar school. During eighth grade, Jerry and a friend went to Chinatown every week. There, they bought firecrackers that they brought back to their school and sold.

Sam and Jerry are upstanding pillars of our community, men of high integrity. Jerry, for example, has had situations in his ownership of sports teams where the lack of a written contract provided opportunity to benefit handsomely. Jerry would not do that, choosing, instead, to live up to the deal, even to his detriment. That's hardly the image of a law breaker.

All entrepreneurs grab opportunities. Some become entrepreneurial before they mature, before they understand that certain opportunities are acceptable and others are not. For Jerry and Sam, entrepreneurship development came early, and the maturity to control it properly didn't follow until later.

Sam Zell was not the only one whose activities with *Playboy* violated the law, and not all of the "law breakers" were kids. Hugh Hefner founded *Playboy* because he saw a demand. There were many magazines, calendars, and posters with pictures of nude women. Hef proposed to repackage sex in wrappings that would be more generally accepted. There were laws in many local communities which not only prevented him from selling the magazine there but also could have caused his arrest. Hefner felt, however, that his timing was right and that the strong desires of the consuming public would change the rules and legalize his activity. He was right.

Sydney Biddle Barrows, the Mayflower Madam, was also catering to the prurient interests of her customers. She, too, tried to repackage sex, in her case by improving the service to the customer and the working conditions of her employees. However, Sydney was plying her packaging on the wrong side of that narrow line and wound up in serious trouble. Of course, Sydney's customers and employees didn't complain about her business practices, the police did.

How do you know which rules or even laws you can break? Although it's perfectly permissible for you to break rules, I strongly recommend that you obey the law. The lesson here is that you can't just memorize which rules are breakable and which are *verboten*. The key is understanding what kinds of rules are "sacred" at a particular time and what kind you can, indeed must, bash if you want to become an entrepreneur.

11

Rules You Gotta Break

Sometimes, you gotta break the rules.
Burger King Restaurant

Rules of the Status Quo

By definition, entrepreneurs break rules, even if only the rules of the status quo. Most entrepreneurs do even more.

Good managers prescribe performance criteria for their employees and reward them for achieving just that measure. Connect all the dots, producing a predetermined pattern, and you win a prize! Entrepreneurs prefer to plot out the dots too. Did I say "prefer"? Actually, it's not a matter of preference at all; they feel compelled to create their own patterns. They have to play the game, like Fast Eddie Felson, the way "nobody's ever played it before," or at least like they've never played it before. Entrepreneurs can't resist breaking several general rules:

1. It can't be done.

2. That's the only way to do it.

3. "They" are the only ones who can do it.

4. Anyone can do it.

"It can't be done" is a virtual invitation to an entrepreneur to prove that "it" can be done. The invitation is even more compelling if others have tried and failed. For example, despite a number of airlines having gone out of business or into bankruptcy recently, several new airlines have been formed.

Profile

Elmer Winter's "Why Not?" Lesson

Overcoming the "It can't be done" syndrome may still require an internal intellectual debate. This debate would be so much easier if your initial and automatic response to "It can't be done" were "Why not?" In this sense, "Why not?" is not really a question but a declaration, "I see no reason why it can't be done, so it can be done."

About three years after Elmer Winter and his partner opened their little Manpower office in Milwaukee, they considered opening an office in Minneapolis. Elmer had the Chamber of Commerce arrange meetings with some Minneapolis businesspeople. He flew up to do some first-hand market research. Every businessperson told Elmer that she or he would not use a temporary help service because no one wants to hire someone who doesn't understand the business well enough. "We're different in Minneapolis," they told him, "Your temporary service won't fly up here." They unanimously declared, "Bringing Manpower to Minneapolis would be a bad idea."

On the flight home, Elmer reviewed his notes carefully. Of course, these reactions were no different from those of the Milwaukee businesspeople who Elmer had interviewed prior to opening the first Manpower office. Next day, he assembled a few of his people and told them, "Look, while the survey indicates that it is not a good idea, let's go ahead anyway."

Now, the rule is that all managers pay attention to market surveys, especially when the results are unanimously negative. How was Elmer able to ignore it, to break the rule? At first, he tried to justify his behavior by claiming that he "was much more of a gut reaction type of person." Then, he related a story about a friend, Cliff Sawdo, who had an interesting background as a jack-of-all-trades and who helped Elmer with his hobby—sculpting large figures by welding used car bumpers.

When Elmer had a seemingly impossible welding job, he would ask Cliff, "How are we gong to do this?" or "Can we really do this?" Sometimes Elmer would get frustrated and say, "There's no way for us to do this." In each instance, Cliff had the same response, "Why not?"

Elmer learned an important lesson from Cliff and now says he always objects to people's initial reactions that you can't do a particular thing or, even worse, that you can't do it because it's never been done before. Elmer always says, "Maybe the times are different or maybe conditions are different or we can approach it differently. Why not give it a try?" And Elmer is convinced that the "Why Not?" attitude is what really helped him start and grow Manpower over the years.

If other people have already proved that it can be done, then you must prove that their way is not the only way to do it. Otherwise, all you can hope for is to be redundant, and entrepreneurs are anything but redundant. Even the business that seems the same as any other is different to its entrepreneur.

If you believe that "they" are the only ones who can do it, then you believe that "they" are giants. Entrepreneurs believe in giants—like Goliath—but they also picture themselves as Davids.

Marketing experts say, if anyone can do it, you might be done in by future competition, so you should reset your sights. Entrepreneurs neither ignore nor are blind to potential competition, but where others see competition, entrepreneurs see opportunities.

In my years representing entrepreneurs and watching them break those rules, I also watched other people fail by not trying; they were not entrepreneurs. Those who tried but couldn't pull it off were. Very few entrepreneurs fail by trying to do something that can't be done; generally, they fail by trying to do things that can't be done at that time, in that particular way, or by that particular person.

Before you break any rules, make sure you understand the

rules and why they exist. There may be a good reason for a customary course of action that has developed into a rule.
Understanding the rules may require time and effort on your
part, but so will cleaning up the mess if you skip that critical step.

Many successful entrepreneurs are so well known for their
flair that you assume that rule breaking is their essence.
Actually, the vast majority of those entrepreneurs honed basic
business skills before striking out on their own, and rule breaking is merely a means of accomplishing their overall goal. Richie
Melman is praised for having more than 30 restaurants, each
with a different theme, decor, and menu. Long before he opened
his first restaurant, he had learned the fundamentals of the
restaurant business by working in his father's deli. Similarly,
Hugh Hefner learned his basics at *Esquire,* Edwin Land at
Kodak, Joe Sullivan at Swift, Harold Geneen at ITT, Edson de
Castro at Digital Equipment, and Thurman Rodgers at
American Microsystems and Advanced Micro Devices. These
entrepreneurs learned the fundamentals on the job, then broke
some rules in applying those basics. They are known for breaking the rules, but had they not developed their fundamental talents, breaking the rules might not have led to success.

Breaking rules seems natural for most entrepreneurs; it is,
after all, a prerequisite if you want to break the shackles of
restrictive behavior and build a new nerve center for your business. Natural, but by no means easy. Even when the basis for
breaking rules is there, strength and determination are needed
to convert rule breaking from a potential liability to an asset.

For the Entrepreneur, Losing Is Winning

George Steinbrenner said, "Show me a good loser, and I'll show
you a loser." I think people who learn from their losses are winners. Entrepreneurs whose projects fail are better entrepreneurs
for their next project. So, even if your business fails, despite or
even because of your thinking or acting differently, learn to convert your being different from a liability to an asset and the
effort will be well worthwhile.

After the failure of the project Thurman Rodgers introduced at American Microsystems, he could have questioned the underlying concept, which was unique. He didn't, and while at Advanced Micro Devices, he observed that marketing was the aspect his project had lacked. He solved his problem by stealing Advanced's marketing man, Lowell Turriff, and adding a different way of marketing to his already unique approach to microchips. His concept only needed that one adjustment to move it from failure to success.

How do you know when you've gone over the line? How can you tell when you have gone from being creative to being creepy or from on the mark to off the wall? Judging yourself is always difficult because self-perception lacks perspective and objectivity. Self-evaluation is made worse by critics, who tend to label anything different as being illegal, offensive, or bizarre. Remember also that those who criticize you when you do different things or do things differently don't understand why you are doing what you are doing and have no insight into your dream. Before you buy the assessment, then, consider the source. Ask these questions about your critics' track records:

Are they in your business?

Are their egos vested in what you would change?

Have they acted differently in their business?

Recently?

Are they predictably critical of change or difference?

Have their prior criticisms been valid?

Look also at what they are critiquing. Are they challenging your idea, your ability to make it work, or the risk involved? Depersonalizing the critique may make it easier to swallow. Imagine that they are critiquing someone else—someone you know but don't thoroughly respect.

If you can't learn much about the critics, then repeat their critiques to someone trustworthy, knowledgeable, and informed, and see how they react. Concentrate on the reasoning behind their reaction, not just their vote. This is not an election or popularity contest; don't get carried away with majority rule. By definition, when you do something different or do it in a new way, you are a minority. In a democratic society, there is a tendency to abide by majority rule. Why, you may ask, should our free enterprise system be any different? If free enterprise were bound to the rule of the majority:

Disney wouldn't exist because the majority of people find mice offensive even when you give them names, and Walt Disney would never have fired his boss.

McDonald's wouldn't exist because, to most people then, thinking that the All-American drive-in could be improved was bizarre, and Ray Kroc would never have fired his boss.

Sara Lee wouldn't exist because "nobody doesn't like" their baked goods fresh, and freezing them would have been bizarre, so Charlie Lubin (Sara Lee's father) would never have fired his boss.

Profile

Howard Schultz's Starbucks: The Tail That Turned the Dog Around

Put down your double espresso or your cafe latte and think about what it was like in 1982: "Regular or decaf, ma'am?" or "Sir, do you need cream or sugar?" That's when Howard Schultz left the large company he was working for in Sweden and went to work in Seattle as marketing director for one of his customers, Starbucks, a small company with four traditional regional stores that sold coffee by the pound, not the cup. A primary reason for joining Starbucks was that the two founders were willing to let Howard earn some equity for his sweat, which meant a lot to Howard. In addition, he saw something in Starbucks. He had a vision about its potential.

Years earlier, while working in Europe, Howard visited Italy, where he was intrigued that there were 200,000 coffee bars in that country and none in America. He tried to paint a picture of the vision, but the Starbuck owners rejected it. He finally convinced them to test it. The test was successful, but they wouldn't roll it out. (Note that Elmer Winter rejected test results and became an entrepreneur, but the two owners of Starbuck rejected test results to avoid an entrepreneurial step.)

So, after three years with Starbucks, Howard left to form his own company. Most potential investors thought his idea was crazy. Howard worked for a year without pay to raise the start-up capital. His wife was pregnant, but Howard had coffee in his roaster. "I was convinced that I was right," he said. Eventually, he raised a million dollars from investors to whom he could illustrate his vision. Sixteen months later, after opening three successful coffee bar stores, he lived the impossible dream. He actually acquired Starbucks. Now, Starbucks has hundreds of stores, opening more each week. The company serves over a million customers a week and is the largest retailer and roaster of special coffee in North America.

In 1982, the rule, that coffee was sold by the pound and not the cup, was gospel—not only to the original owners of Starbucks but also to most of the people whose investments Howard sought. I asked Howard how he knew that he was right and they were wrong and that the rule could be broken.

"I don't think you ever know you are right," Howard told me, "but I felt passionately that the social aspect of coffee was a conduit to conversation and that coffee bars, such as those I saw in Italy, created a meeting place and a new lifestyle that would work in America." Howard wasn't just concerned with his financial dilemma (pregnant wife, no job, no prospects); he was concerned that, in his small community, breaking a rule that couldn't be broken ("Wake up and smell the coffee, Son, this is America, not Italy. Go get a serious job and support your family.") would be a public embarrassment.

Some people say Howard was lucky that it worked, that the rule could be broken. Howard responded by reminding me of Branch Rickey's line, "Luck is the residue of design."

There is a great similarity between our democratic form of government and our free enterprise system. Both involve majority rule (marketplace demand in the case of free enterprise), but, with each, its essence lies in the protection of those who differ with the majority. Within reasonable limits, our system fosters uniqueness by recognizing and rewarding the value it adds. So, remember, it's OK to be different. The only time being different is bad is when you allow it to prevent you from implementing your dream. So, get going. To be an entrepreneur, you must do something different or do things differently. Avoid doing anything truly illegal, offensive, or bizarre, and measure the critics and critiques so you can know whether you've gone too far. But don't be afraid of being different. And don't worry about breaking some rules (not laws). Your traditions should be your inspirations, not your limitations.

12

Dealing with Past Failure

The past is prologue.
Engraved on the U.S. Supreme Court
Building

Parables are society's attempt to teach us to learn from past mistakes. We deal with the calamitous events of world history by looking back, remembering, and, then, armed with the wisdom learned from the lessons of the past, moving forward. Some people never stop to look back at their failures. Maybe it's easier to review history and other people's mistakes than to look at our own mistakes. Reviewing other people's mistakes may be fine for teaching us general lessons, but revisiting our own is more important because we not only avoid repeating them but also heal old wounds that might inhibit us from trying again.

Failure destroys confidence. But, by looking at failure as a positive experience—learning from your mistakes in order to be wiser next time—your confidence can be salvaged.

It's OK to fail. Failing shouldn't be a goal, but it is necessary for most of us to succeed. That's a hard lesson to learn. Nothing makes you feel as stupid as making wrong decisions, unless you're as smart as Sam LeFrak. When I asked Sam to what he attributes his success, he said, "Two words: *right decisions*." Then I asked him how to make right decisions, and Sam answered, "One word: *experience.*" The next question, of course, was how he got experience. Sam responded, "Two words: *wrong decisions.*"

But I've Never Failed

Howard Ruff lost all he had and went deeply into debt when his business failed. Yet, he says, "I look back at what I lost back then and stack that up against all I kept or gained (referring to knowledge, not cash). It wasn't a big deal."

Ruff says, "Maybe it will take two or three failures before you get it right." He referred to those experiences as "incidents" or "episodes," which assume proper perspective when compared to the events of a lifetime. Ruff's "episodes" are reminders and motivators, which, according to Ruff, never "determine the tone for the whole rest of your life."

Otto Clark's program—to sell millions of copy machines in China—failed. Otto said, if you "failed yesterday, you pick up your pieces in the morning. Every morning is a new process with new opportunities you didn't have yesterday."

Whether you call your setbacks bad decisions, bad experiences, episodes, incidences, or processes, or even if you admit they are failures, you can learn from them and prevent them from interfering with tomorrow's "new process."

Obstacles cause failure, but they themselves are not failures. Entrepreneurs cannot study their failures, if they don't believe they failed, but they can study the obstacles to their success in order to deal with them correctly next time. So, learn to recognize the past impediments; then, when you encounter them again you can deal with them. That gives you two areas to study—the way you deal with the setback and the obstacles that caused them, and neither exercise requires that you admit to failure.

No one wants to fail. Many managers, in an attempt to avoid failure, ignore opportunities that appear risky. Because they worry about always making the right decisions, according to Sam LeFrak, managers often deprive themselves of the potential rewards of experiences. Entrepreneurs, however, like a risky ride. They don't plan on failing but are willing to accept the risk of failure if that's what it takes to achieve their goal. What happens when managers do fail? Does the experience transform them into entrepreneurs?

Christie Hefner, the CEO of Playboy, entered the business world believing "that failure was a terrible thing to do." She's smart, a quick study, and she chose her parents well, so she was quickly elevated to top management at the company her father, Hugh Hefner, started. The company was in trouble, struggling to survive. Christie had no choice. If she and Playboy were to succeed, she had to become more than a manager, she had to use entrepreneurial skills. She couldn't just airbrush Playboy's exposed parts, she had to remake its central nervous system.

Playboy had become an institution, and institutions don't change easily. In addition, any change by Christie might have been considered criticism of her father. Worst of all, mistakes would ruin her image, and she had worked so hard to gain her stature. Nevertheless, Christie closed traditional profit centers and moved Playboy into new ventures, new businesses. She drove Playboy over the rough roads leading to her vision of where the company should be. Her vision was fixed, so the rough road became necessary and, therefore, no barrier. However, that meant adopting a new perspective on failure, accepting those experiences as "not so terrible," and viewing them as lessons that would improve her future decisions.

A number of successful entrepreneurs I've represented and interviewed had prior businesses that had failed. Those entrepreneurs told me they never failed. They felt that way because they learned and became better entrepreneurs as a result of their experiences. They dealt with the very failures that "never happened to them."

Profile

Andrew Filipowski Sees Failure as Part of the Initiation Rite

When you read about Andrew Filipowski, whose nickname is "Flip," you might think that it stands for flippant, but I can assure you that is not the case.

After World War II, Flip's parents immigrated from Poland to Chicago, where they ran a small ethnic neighborhood grocery store behind which they lived. Flip now knows that they were poor, but he grew up thinking his lot in life was normal. To make sure he grew up an American, Flip's mother worked and skimped to put him through a Catholic military school, which, according to Flip, typically housed rich kids, disciplinary cases, and even kids from mafia families. His father, a former Polish general, repeatedly advised Flip, "If you are poor, you are stupid. If you are stupid, you are poor."

Flip dropped out of college and learned the newly emerging computer technology at a series of jobs with large corporations. His last job provided a stock option plan which gave Flip the nest egg to start his own company. He took in a partner and started to grow the business.

"I can't stand losing," Flip told me, "I've never been able to. I have a healthy attitude and a bad one at the same time. I hate it. I have a momentary emotional explosion of great anger aimed at myself, of incredible pain, and then an immediate shut down of that feeling. When I lose, I go through an immediate 15 minutes of overwhelming anger. Then that's over with and it's a new chapter."

Quick rebound has helped Flip through some trying times, like the time Flip fired his partner. His partner immediately sided with Shamrock, the major venture capital shareholder in Flip's business. Together, they ousted Flip, who was greeted by armed guards when he arrived at work. Flip was advised to take legal action and to take six months off and organize his life to get over it. But such advice was too late. Flip felt tremendous sadness, anger, and depression, but only momentarily. Fewer than 24 hours later, Flip had founded Platinum Technologies, the company he's since taken public which is currently valued in 9 digits. Flip feels that in those 24 hours, he became an entrepreneur.

In Flip's view, failing is a prerequisite. According to Flip, "nobody is worth their salt unless they have been down on the mat, down and out, knocked out, and get up and win. The only people worth respecting are those who have gone through that experience. With the guys who haven't failed, you really never know if they could handle that. They are not quite up to snuff."

Trying entrepreneurship a second time, after a less-than-successful first try, seemed natural to Flip (it was part of his 24-hour initiation to the entrepreneurs' club), even though he told me, "If you screw up twice, you are really finished." With that elevated sense of risk on the second go-around, why did Flip do it?

The morning of the day Platinum was born, he told himself, "the world is filled with idiots who every day of their life say 'I'm going to do it, I'm going to do it,' and they never do it, for whatever reason or excuse they use. I was going to do it."

That morning, Flip was in the shower and had an "incredible gnawing pain." He was sweating profusely, realizing that he was risking his house, his kids' educations, everything, so he could have his own business. He thought of every excuse not to, but he knew he had to have his own business. Most important, he realized that he loved the feeling he was experiencing. He wanted to have that feeling for the rest of his life. He relished the panic, because "if you can control this panic, you can do anything."

Flip feels that the major rush he has that gets him going every day is the constant reminder that he could fail, and that if he did fail, he'd hate it. By the same token, he saw his first failure as a rite of passing. I think that if he failed again, he'd view it and deal with it the same way.

Entrepreneurs are special; they can, as the song says, pick themselves up, dust themselves off, and start all over again. In other words, they aren't stopped by the failure of something they did. Entrepreneurs may not be affected by the past failure itself, but they are molded by what they learn from how they dealt with past failures.

The Appropriate Mourning Period and Suitable Memorial

Religious principles and traditions guide the length of time we spend mourning lost loved ones. To entrepreneurs, their dream is their love. How long should they mourn its loss and what is a suitable memorial?

Don Boroian went through a bankruptcy in 1982 after pouring a second half-million dollars into a company he had acquired for half a million dollars. He had guaranteed the debt with his main company, so he lost everything. This was not the first of Don's businesses to fail, but now Don was older. The business supported Don and his two sons, as well as valued and loyal employees. Don had no second thoughts about restarting the business, and he subscribed to no mourning period. Don says he started planning for the new business while the old business was "still in its smoldering ashes and maybe even while it was still in flames."

Don't Confuse Me with the Facts

As long as you're looking back, you might as well do it right; you might as well get the facts straight. When you look at a prior failure, you must be objective, cold-hearted, and even cruel. You must see the failure and its causes as they really were. You are better off doing that early, before developing a new passion that would have to be interrupted. In any event, it needs to be done; otherwise, the experience will be wasted, and you will continue to make wrong decisions instead of right ones. Here are some lessons that will help.

Make Tracks before You Look Back

Gary Greenberg and his partner, Sheldon Stillman, have been in the airline food business for more than 20 years. Gary says they have never failed but admits they've "made mistakes" and tried to learn from them. That's not very novel for an entrepreneur, but Gary's analysis of *when* to do it is.

Gary observed that he and his partner don't linger over "making a mistake" to determine what they will do differently next time. Instead, they move right on to the next dream, until they are just about "ready to make that decision," and then say, "What did we learn from the last time?" That's different from what most entrepreneurs say they do. Most are like Lester Crown, the multibillionaire owner of General Dynamics and many other companies, who tries to study his mistakes right away. Lester feared that waiting until later would lead to rationalizing. Others believe that waiting removes you from the failure, reduces the need to personalize it, and promotes much-needed objectivity.

There's a lot of wisdom in Gary's observation. At the time of the mistake, you may be too close to the situation to be objective. This was, after all, your dream, your baby. It's difficult, during or just after your dream period, to see and say what was wrong. Even more important, by immediately moving forward and stopping to look back only later, you develop an immediate momentum of going forward, which helps prevent the prior experience from immobilizing you or, worse yet, pulling you back. If you stick around to conduct the autopsy of your business failure, you might miss a window of opportunity.

Separate Yourself from the Failure

People who were once involved in a failure tend to view themselves and the failure as one and the same. That's wrong. You and your failure are not identical, and you must learn to view them separately.

Gary Greenberg couldn't have moved on unless he were able to separate himself from the failure, because his prior failure was an anchor that was an immovable object which would have deflated Gary's force. The same could happen to you. If you see yourself back at the failure, you will view yourself as a failure just when you foresee your next dream, and that can deprive you of your next chance. As you sail for your dream, keep your eyes on the horizon, not the rocky shore behind.

Don't Make Excuses

Howard Ruff told me, "You've only failed when you've given up or when you've blamed someone else." Blaming someone or something else is a cancer. Once you introduce that excuse into your system, it will consume you entirely. The cancer is sometimes difficult to recognize. The customary phrases, "It was Joe's fault, not mine" or "It was caused by the recession; I couldn't help it" are not the only way these excuses are expressed. Some people are more subtle, using phrases like "If only" and "But for." Those phrases are more dangerous because they make it more difficult to realize you're using excuses.

The world is filled with external forces—other people, fate, and acts of God—which are easy to use as excuses. Those interruptions should not become your excuses; they are facts of life which you must learn to anticipate, meet, and overcome if you want to succeed. Those things happen and, sometimes, are unavoidable and overwhelming. Succumbing to such forces doesn't make you a failure, even though it may prevent your succeeding. But to use external forces as excuses, instead of letting the experiences teach you how to do better the next time, is to fail. You'll never be ready to make your next venture a success if you are still using excuses and blaming your mistakes on others. Only when you learn nothing from your experience are you a failure.

The S.O.B. Story

You may accept intellectually what I say about not using excuses, but you're going to tell me emotionally that things were different in the circumstances of your failure. You're not blaming someone else as an excuse, you'll say, but some S.O.B. really screwed things up. That doesn't wash with me.

In almost every failure, there's an S.O.B., either a man or a woman, someone whose behavior, attitude, or mere presence contributed to the failure. I'd hate to tell you how many times I've heard about "that S.O.B." who caused the deal to fail. I've heard it from clients and prospective clients, as well as from other entrepreneurs who were promoting deals to our venture capital clients. Sure, there really are S.O.B.s in the world, and they certainly can cause failure. But don't blame them. Most often, they are scapegoats; "S.O.B.," in their case, stands for "scapegoats of blame." Even when they are real S.O.B.s, you must be able to deal effectively with them if you want to be a successful entrepreneur.

Richie Melman is known as the restauranteur with the Midas touch. He has founded more than 30 restaurants and has an astounding survival record, with his closings being limited to a loss of lease and a fire. Yet, Richie has had failures. At the request of the Hefners, he took over operations of the faltering Playboy Clubs. A year later, they all closed. Several other restaurants his company contracted to manage also didn't succeed. There was ample opportunity for Richie to blame others—in his case, the owners who set the rules for Richie to follow. However, when I asked Richie what went wrong, he didn't accuse the owners. He recognized his own fault, "I respect people who have money. I agreed to do it their way, even though I thought it was wrong." Not only did Richie Melman avoid blaming others, he understood the reason behind his failure to deal effectively with them.

When you look back, separate the S.O.B. from the way you feel about him (or her). Treat him as another external force and figure out how you could have dealt with him. If he was really an S.O.B., maybe you had to be a bigger one. If he was really more talented than you, maybe you should have skipped that "opportunity." There's always a solution. You must figure out, now, how you could have won then, so you'll know how to win next time.

Know What Signals You Missed

"If you have to wait for the numbers to find out whether you're in trouble, then it's probably too late." That's important advice from Columbia Business School Professor John O'Whitney. Every business has signals that serve as vital warnings that something is wrong. The entrepreneur's job is to look for them, to recognize what he sees, and to do something to improve the situation.

Consider the ultimate start-up situation, where the entrepreneur conceives of a new product to solve an existing problem or satisfy a current need. The research and development (R&D) stage, projected for a certain period, will then be followed by marketing and manufacturing. Murphy's Law is a full-time resident in R&D projects. As things go wrong in R&D and its time extends, that is a signal. The entrepreneur must see that the delay means (1) capital is being consumed, (2) if the solution wasn't perfect, maybe the problem was misperceived, (3) competitors may be catching up or pulling ahead, and (4) original plans for marketing and manufacturing may be outmoded. Eventually, the results of the delay will be apparent in the numbers, but by then it may be too late.

Unfortunately, many start-up jockeys focus so intently on the dream that they don't hear or see the signal until it is transcribed into their language. You must meet the signals early; you must see them in the raw stage.

See What Blinded You

It's not enough to recognize that you missed critical signals; you also must know why you missed them. There are many possible reasons—lack of experience or training, insufficient research and due diligence, diversions due to lack of capital, poor planning, and, the most typical reason, love.

Remember what made you jump in and take the plunge? You cast aside all the fears, myths, and excuses and took the big leap, because *you believed* in your dream and yourself and *you wanted* to be independent or in control and in charge of your destiny. You selected your particular business because you were supposed to choose something *you knew and loved*. Love—yes; smitten blind—no! Know the difference.

There are many reasons for the high number of divorces recently. One big reason is a failure of one party to see the other party for what he or she really is. An even bigger reason is the failure of both parties to see themselves. The same is true for entrepreneurs. Some are blinded by their dream; most are blinded by their egos. There's plenty of time for pride later, when you can look back at success. There's no room for ego when you're still looking forward. Know and understand whatever blinded you the last time. Plan how to avoid that pitfall.

13
Prepare for the Opportunity

If you build it, he will come.

Field of Dreams

By now, you know what an entrepreneur is and what you have to do to become one—how to dream, what to do with your dream, how to buy it, sell it, focus on it, stick with it, and convert it to reality. Remember the words on old bumper stickers that say, "If you're so smart, why ain't you rich?" You now know what's needed. The next step is to get the lead out and do it.

I had a mentor problem. I respected and admired my boss who had been a great mentor; as a matter of fact, too great. My partner and I discussed the prospect of starting our own firm. We agreed that the legal profession presented huge opportunities for those who would start the kind of firm we proposed. I hesitated because I decided that, at 28 years old, I was not adequately prepared. I felt tied to my mentor; I was convinced that I had much more to learn and much more preparation to do before I'd be able to take on the opportunity of my own firm. Nine months later, I decided I was ready. Trust me, during those nine months, I didn't gain a lifetime of knowledge and experience in the law, which would have constituted preparation for the opportunity of the business itself. In those months, however, I did learn how to prepare for the opportunity.

I began to appreciate the role confidence plays in achieving success during that nine months after first meeting my partner. I recognized that I didn't have to be totally prepared on day one to run a big law firm and professional practice. I just had to have the momentum and trajectory to be ready for future tests and targets. The night before we opened our office, I slept well. I knew that what counted was the rate of progress I was making, not the stage I was at. That night, I knew I wasn't ready to run a big law firm but I knew how far I had progressed in those nine months and that I was ready to continue to learn from my own experience. That made getting started easy.

Prepare as an Actor Does

An Actor Prepares, by Constantin Stanislavsky, explains and teaches the process known as "method acting." That was the technique I used during those nine months before founding my firm. While working for my boss and mentor, I wasn't in a position to be in the driver's seat and to see, first hand, how good I might be. But I could pretend I was in the driver's seat. I could decide what I would do if I were in control. Then, I could compare my decisions and my hypothetical action to my mentor's. That's exactly what I did, and it didn't take long for me to realize that I'd be ready for the real challenges.

Getting Ready to Get Ready

Joe Sullivan lived in a society filled with opportunities. In his decades at Swift and Esmark, he saw his chairman, Donald Kelly, and others seize innumerable openings. While promising situations abounded, Joe strived to be prepared. He knew he had sufficient knowledge and experience in the food and agricultural industries, but he struggled to be properly positioned, financially and emotionally, when the time came to leave his long-time boss.

You must prepare before the occasions arise. Don't wait for a clean stage to come along and then try to prepare yourself for its challenges. Don't waste valuable time getting ready when you should be dealing with the opening. If you're worrying about your level of preparedness when lightning strikes, you will be too preoccupied. You will be a creature of preparedness, when you should be a creature of opportunity.

I don't mean to imply that you must be completely prepared for everything. If you always wait until you are fully prepared, you convert preparedness from a tool to an excuse. If you happen to be prepared totally when a suitable situation arrives, fine. If you're only partially ready, fine, too, because with some extra effort, you can make it. That extra effort comes after the fact, by which time you've already become a creature of opportunity.

The preparatory work you do before the opportunity arrives involves increasing your business knowledge and capability. The work you do after should relate to implementing the opportunity—seeing it and seizing it. When you learn to play golf, you practice endlessly to perfect your swing, so that in a real match you don't have to think about the swing but can, instead, concentrate on subtleties. The same is true for entrepreneurial opportunities. Practice endlessly before the opportunities arise, and when they come you won't have to think about preparing and can concentrate on taking advantage of them.

Many entrepreneurs have been preparing all their lives. Some as boys and girls had paper routes. Or they have mowed lawns, babysat, or done errands for the neighbors. The list is endless. Sue Ling Gin was a Chinese American who began her preparation as a preteen in a middle America town.

Profile

Sue Ling Gin and This Old House: A Moving Experience

Sue Ling Gin's father owned a Chinese-American restaurant in Aurora, Illinois. But he died when Sue Ling was ten. Her mother was a homemaker who had always worked at home. She spoke very little English. Sue Ling started work a year later—in the family restaurant. "My 'uncle' then owned the restaurant and ran it."

"The Chinese have extended families. Uncles aren't necessarily blood uncles, but they come from the same region," Sue Ling says and adds, "They carry the same last name and, in many ways, they treat you as an uncle would in a regular family."

Sue Ling was cashier and used to make the hectograph menus. They would seem quite primitive in today's world of letter quality menus from laser printers. Sue Ling would type the menu on a master sheet using an indelible purple ink. The master was placed on a flat bed of gelatin for a time and the ink would sink into the surface. Then she placed menu sheets face down on the gelatin to make copies.

Pay was substandard. When she was 12 or 13 she quit, moving into a larger immigrant community to work at the Bit of Sweden restaurant. Her job was to fill the smorgasbord table. She got 25 cents more an hour. Her mother was supportive, even though Sue Ling was breaking away from her heritage. According to Sue Ling, "She's kind of a stoic woman. You can usually guess her approval by the look that she has, and many times you don't know if it's an approval or not. It's up to you to figure it out."

Sue Ling continued to work all through high school, buying her own clothes, paying for her books, her pencils, and other mundane items. Her last two summers in high school she went to Chicago, where she worked two jobs. That final summer, after she graduated from high school and was headed for DePaul University, she paid a visit to her mother and her brother in Aurora.

Sue Ling was 17 and her brother was nearly ten years older. They were walking down the street by a certain corner in town that was slated to become a Shell gasoline station. At the time, there was a clapboard house standing on that corner.

"My brother and I thought we'd go take a look at it and see if there were any goodies that we could take home, since they were going to tear it down anyway.

"So we looked in it and we both kind of looked at each other and said, you know, it's a real shame that this house has to be torn down. He said, 'I think we could do something with this house.' So he contacted a friend who sold him an empty lot."

Together they went to the Shell real estate man and offered to pay $2000 for the house. "He was very happy to see us, because it was going to cost him $3000 to tear the house down. In his mind, he thought he made $5000 that day.

For $3000, they ended up with a building and a lot. They put in a foundation for roughly $4500 and had a contractor put the house on flatbeds and move it into the street and through the town, then place it on the foundation at the new lot.

Then the two went to the bank and borrowed $18,000. "We used the money to remodel the house into six apartments. My brother owns it to this day."

This was Sue Ling's first entrepreneurial venture. But it wasn't her last. She used her early restaurant training in her own restaurant, and, in time, she set up a catering service that provides airline meals called Flying Food Fare. Midway Airlines was her best customer. When the airline failed, her business was hit hard. But she is still the optimistic entrepreneur. She comments: "You've got to fail four times in order to get to the fifth time, and the fifth time's going to succeed."

Stoke Your Furnace; Close Your Other Vents

If your furnace heats your whole house and you want to make the bedroom warmer, you can either boost the energy level by turning up the furnace or close the other vents or radiators, concentrating the heat into the bedroom. Or, of course, you can do both. Then, you're really cookin'.

The same directions can guide a new venture. If you want to embark on the road to entrepreneurship, stoke up your energy level and close off all your other outlets, concentrating your new high energy level on being your own boss.

You've heard stories about ordinary people who gain extraordinary strength during emergencies—people who lift a car to save a loved one. They build super energy through a rush of adrenalin and focus it into one act, closing off all other outlets. That's what entrepreneurs do. They have a task so vital that energy and focus become almost natural. In fact, they feed on each other. The more you focus the application of your energy, the more excitement and energy you will create. That's what happened when I started my firm. My rush of energy enabled my sleep requirements to shrink from 8 to 3 or 4 hours, without feeling tired. A similar rush of energy is experienced by all entrepreneurs. Although most get more than 4 hours of sleep, they generally sleep less than they did before and feel less tired. Entrepreneurs also focus their energy, which makes them even more productive.

In his book, *Financing and Investing in Private Companies*, Arthur Lipper, III, says he can always spot entrepreneurs in an airport—they're the ones who walk fast because they have no time to waste and no one to pay for any wasted time. Of course, Arthur may not know whether they are racing to a departing flight or to a pit stop.

Making the Journey's First Step Easy

The first step in every journey is the longest and hardest step. For most entrepreneurs, the first step is easier than it is for others, because they are already walking. By the time they're confronted with the "first step," they have momentum. For them, the first step is the middle of their journey. Gertrude Crain told me how her husband, G. D. Crain, started the publication *Advertising Age* during the Depression. Eventually, that grew to be Crain Communications, with over 25 successful publications. She remembered G. D. saying that, "if he had known how tough it would be to get business, maybe he would have thought twice about it." He had thought about the business for a long time in advance of founding it; his advance preparation made his starting *Advertising Age* seem easier than it was, like the middle of his journey.

If you understand what G. D. Crain did, you've discovered the secret. If your entrepreneurship embarkation starts well before that difficult first step, then the "first step" that is so difficult for others will be a cinch for you.

Once you have prepared to get ready, you must take some active first steps to run your business. Here are three points of information to help you do that.

Point of Information

Choosing the Right Partner: It's a Marriage

Should you have a partner? Andrew "Flip" Filipowski told me, "you usually pick a partner to help you suffer the losses. You very rarely pick a partner to share the successes with." When I congratulated Jerry Reinsdorf on his wisdom in buying the Chicago Bulls just before Michael Jordan came on the scene, he half jokingly commented on his own bad judgment for taking in partners on such a successful venture.

It's a lot like sailing. It's nice to have a sailing partner to absorb certain tasks, to relieve you when you're tired, to teach you what you don't know, and to correct your errors (if you believe you can err), but nothing quite matches the exhilaration of having done it all alone. A sailing partner may rescue you if you fall overboard. Of course, if you do take a partner in sailing, his or her mistake could capsize you. The same is true in business. You could face personal bankruptcy because of your or your partner's acts.

Once you decide to take a partner, you've also decided that you are willing to give up a degree of control over your business. But that's not necessarily bad news. The right partner can give you the confidence to be more entrepreneurial than otherwise. If you choose well, the partner will complement your talents. Thus, the business will have a better chance of success. If you are lucky enough to have a partnership that combines these virtues, one and one will add up to more than two.

I can't stress this enough: You must find the right partner. Follow these rules in that quest:

1. Where you find your partner varies.
    a. An inordinately large number are spouses. Several ingredients critical to a good partnership—trust, respect, comfort in dealing and being together—already exist and have been tested in the marriage. Debbi Fields made one hell of a chocolate chip cookie and had the glamour and personality to sell her cookies to everyone. And her husband, Randy Fields, had the business talent and the

ability to develop systems that enabled expansion to
hundreds of stores. Jenny Craig and her husband,
Sid; Eileen Ford and her husband, Jerry; and Gordon
Segal and his wife, Carol, are other examples of mates for
fun and profit.

b. Some find partners in nonmarital best friends. Judd
Malkin selected his college roommate, Neill Bluhm, to
start JMB. So did Sam Zell, with his college friend,
the late Bob Lurie (better than sharing a room, they shared
ownership of whole buildings while still in college).
And the friendship leading to the successful business
relationship of Ben & Jerry is well-known.

c. Often, partners worked together at their prior job. Gary
Greenberg and Sheldon Stillman formed Sage
Enterprises after their prior boss disincentivized them.
Dennis Keller and Ronald Taylor worked together at Bell
& Howell before they acquired the DeVry Institute.
Howard Schultz worked for Starbucks before he became
a partner with its owners, whom he later bought out
to pursue his blend for brewing the business.

d. If your spouse, best friend, and coworkers don't fit,
your options are far from exhausted. Those very people,
who know your needs and quirks, may have good
insight as to prospective partners. Mutual friends
introduce many business partners. That's how I met the
fellow who cofounded my firm. Your lawyer and
accountant also may know of people with similar goals
and complementary talents. So, too, your mentor may be
a mentor to someone else. If you are active in trade or
professional associations, you may spot suitable
candidates there.

2. Make an assessment of any potential partner's talents and his
or her capacity for growth. Then take an objective inventory
of your own talents and capacity for growth. If you are the
creative or sales talent, look for someone to run the production
and financial end. Incidentally, don't confuse marketing
(devising a plan for selecting and contacting the potential
market) with sales (getting in the customer's door and
walking out with an order). Sometimes, the assessment is

pretty basic. Judd Malkin selected Neill Bluhm because Neill was the smartest person Judd had ever met.

3. Consider the business's needs now and in the future to the best of your ability. As a business grows and matures, its needs change. Selecting a partner who fills start-up needs but won't fill future needs can be short-sighted. The result can be carrying a partner's dead weight, which leaves no room for a new partner who could be productive in the growing business.

4. Check the references of prospective partners, especially with their former partners, if any. Recognize that past associates of your prospective partner might fear that honest, negative comments could subject them to a lawsuit. So when possible, use intermediaries who are close to your source and who may get a better reading than you can manage as a stranger.

5. Make sure that you deal openly with your prospective partner about your priorities. Don't forget, you must sell your potential partner on the prospects for your dream without building false expectations which could backfire. It is also critical that you learn what your partner is like. So listen and compare what he or she says to what the references say.

Define the partnership. You should decide up-front how you will deal with the apparent conflicts between you and your partner, and you should set up a general procedure for dealing with the unanticipated conflicts. A good lawyer, experienced in helping entrepreneurial partnerships, can help you flesh out your list of and consider possible conflict areas.

Partnership means different things to different people. Your partner may wish or be willing to remain silent and cede control to you. Of course, an investor who provides capital or critically important talent may demand to be a full partner, and then you might draft your partnership agreement so you share control.

Sometimes, an investor will insist on the majority piece. Try offering a portion of your profits and equity in lieu of voting rights. Or arrange for a phantom stock program or grant stock without voting rights for a period of time. Or, even tie in the right to buy back the shares at a predetermined or formula-driven price after a given number of years.

One of the principal reasons for becoming an entrepreneur was to control and determine your own destiny. So it is natural that you want to control your business. However, if your efforts to wrest voting control fail, all is not lost. Real control comes from doing so well that you seem indispensable. Of course, no one really is. But you can make yourself very difficult to replace. Just don't hurt the business in doing so.

Don't get me wrong—being valuable and seeming indispensable is a pragmatic back-up position where you can't otherwise secure voting control. Voting control is preferable, as Andrew "Flip" Filipowski learned. Flip selected a partner in his prior business, DBMS, and they brought in a venture capital group that included Roy Disney. Flip became a minority shareholder, and, one day, he arrived at his office to find armed guards who prevented his entry and informed him that he was history at DBMS. Before you say "poor Flip," you should know that, more recently, Flip founded Platinum Technologies, a software company he took public. Flip's compensation last year approximated $13 million, and the market value of his stock is in nine figures. But you may not be as fortunate as Flip, you may not get a second good opportunity, so cover yourself the first time.

However you take on a partner, whole or lesser, real or phantom, early or late, try hard to structure the agreement so your partner will be fully motivated.

Do a reality check. The number one problem in partnerships is unrealistic expectations. Make sure you and you partner aren't starry-eyed over prospects.

Point of Information

Format: Corporate or What?

You should construct a form for your business that comes as close as possible to fitting your needs. The form of organization you use to set up your business is a type of insurance against certain worst-case scenarios and a type of tool for simplifying and reducing the cost of operating your business.

This is a totally different issue than whether you choose to go it alone or take a partner. The right business format can provide you with a way to limit liability, to safeguard your nonbusiness assets, and to facilitate your sailing into another business should your first one end in a visit to bankruptcy court. Consider using some kind of corporate format—business corporation, closely held corporation, limited liability company, a limited partnership with a corporate general partner, or a general partnership with corporate general partners—so that you can float to safety even if your boat sinks to the bottom.

Not that corporations are a panacea. Your bank probably will demand that you personally guarantee repayment of the money that it lends your corporation. Your landlord and even certain suppliers may do the same. You might protect your personal finances from such a guarantee, if your estate plan calls for transfer of your assets to a friendly parent, spouse, or child or, better yet, a family partnership, domestic trust, or foreign-situs trust. The form and timing of such a transfer and the nature of your disclosures to the bank will determine the success of this procedure; professional guidance is critical. The bank may require the guarantee of such a transferee, if they realize what you have done, but you may get away with a partial guaranty by the transferee or sometimes none at all. Then, if your business succeeds, you should refinance without any guarantee as soon as possible.

What if your transferees are friendly but not trustworthy? What if, for whatever reason, you don't trust your spouse or you are divorced but have a great relationship with your kids? Even if, in those circumstances, you can trust your children, how do you feel about your mate's or exmate's influence over the kids? And even if your spouse's influence is of no concern, I have seen what happens when parents place big bucks in their kids' names. They often create "heir heads." How you deal with this is a personal matter. But, deal with it you must.

Also, there are costs involved in forming and being a corporation, including professional fees, possibly taxes, and internal formalities. It's like an insurance premium. After all, even life jackets cost something.

So exactly what structure do you use? Before you decide, I

suggest that you keep three main goals for your business structure constantly in mind. You must:

1. *Limit your liability.* There is no need to expose everything you own, your house, your car, investments, and art collection to the risks of your business. As an entrepreneur you want to be savvy and smart, not macho and mistaken.

2. *Avoid double taxation.* If a corporation earns money, it pays income taxes. If the money is then distributed as dividends it is taxed again—to the shareholders. There are those non-corporate structures that are not subject to the double tax. But as I've already indicated, some of them will expose your personal assets to creditors.

3. *Keep it simple.* Reconciling those two goals—limiting your liability and avoiding double taxation—may create a complex structure that muddles your business operations. This shortcoming can outweigh the benefits.

Remember that whatever structure you select, you must be sure to motivate the people in your business. The structure with the most appeal to outside investors may be a partnership, which would let them recoup their capital before any earnings (over and above salaries) are distributed to the entrepreneurs. A different structure, such as a corporation with a nonqualified profit-sharing plan or a limited partnership where employees can own or earn limited partner units, might provide liquid rewards to employees. Meanwhile, a corporation, with a stock option plan or possibly a phantom stock plan, could bring forth exceptional efforts on the part of employees since they would own "a piece of the rock." Before you discuss the selection of an entity with your lawyer and accountant, you need a general understanding of the alternatives.

Corporations provide limited liability. They are the traditional entity for eventually taking a company public. Public companies gain liquidity and get objective outside valuation. Both qualities can help attract key personnel and serious capital. You will probably start with one of these limited liability corporations favored by start-ups:

C corporations are regular corporations, taxed at the corporate level, creating potential double taxation. For closely held companies where compensation consumes all income, double taxation becomes irrelevant. With this structure you will have the maximum flexibility to create devices that will be useful in motivating the employees of the company.

S corporations are also regular corporations, but you can elect to skip the corporate-level tax. In turn, shareholders are taxed on all corporate income, regardless of whether it is distributed. Stockholders must be U.S. individuals, and the stock is limited to one class, preventing many substructures that are useful for motivating employees. Also, if the entrepreneur is to receive stock free, or for less money than other investors, structure and tax considerations become more complex.

Partnerships avoid double taxation in essentially the same way that S corporations do, without limitations as to the types of owners or the classes of participation and with greater flexibility for investors to recoup capital before distribution of earnings. But these advantages may not justify some of the attendant risks.

General partnerships leave partners exposed for business liabilities, including those incurred by other partners. This format is too risky for individuals, unless they have no choice. Professionals, for example, may not be allowed to avoid personal liability to clients through incorporation. Partnerships are most useful for joint ventures between companies, each of which sets up a subsidiary corporation (enjoying limited liability) to serve as a partner in the general partnership.

Limited partnerships can restrict the liability of limited partner investors, if those limited partners are not active in the business. But there must be a general partner who is active and who risks substantial personal assets, either individually or through a substantially capitalized corporate general partner.

Limited liability corporations are a relatively new concept that combine the limited liability and structure advantages of a C corporation with the tax benefits of a partnership. This structure is not permitted in all states. Where it does apply, it can help a locally operated business that doesn't meet S corporation requirements to limit liability, while enabling unique income, dividend, or stock ownership allocations.

Keep these caveats in mind:

1. Your needs may change. If so, you may have to switch to a new form of business entity. Such changes can be problematic if you have partners who would be adversely affected or if the changes increase taxes.

2. These formations are subject to complex rules which change frequently and which require technical interpretation. Do not proceed without the help of qualified professionals.

Point of Information

Advisors: The Right Stuff

As George Orwell would put it, some business professionals are more equal than others. One place to start is with professionals who have experience working with entrepreneurs.

Outside Professionals

Accountant.   Let's start with your accountant. Virtually every business must have an accountant, most probably on a continuing basis. Good accountants help clients stay out of trouble. They interpret numbers, highlighting the procedures that need to be corrected. Accountants can help you do basic bookkeeping and cost accounting. They can set up controls and create a cost accounting system for your business. They perform audits for publicly owned companies and fill other needs for smaller businesses. They offer advice on tax planning, fill out your tax returns, and serve as your advocate at the IRS.

Accountants can also give you credibility. If you have no track record as a businessperson, you might consider hiring a well-known regional or even one of the big six accounting firms, particularly so if you must raise serious money.

But most start-up or small entrepreneurial businesses require more personalized attention. You should consider either smaller firms or the small business/entrepreneur department of a large firm. They are more familiar with and more often willing to answer business questions. They are likely to be more aggressive for you in their interpretations of tax matters, for example. They usually charge lower fees per hour or at least gear their services to the more limited needs of your size business. You are more likely to be one of their bigger clients early on, which makes you more important and deserving of better service. Make sure that the man or woman assigned to handle your business, not just the firm as a whole, is top notch. Try to gauge the accountant's personal professional experience and select one who has been through it before so you can benefit by what the accountant has learned from larger clients who have been through all you are facing. Decide what you need and choose accordingly.

Insurance Consultant. This may surprise you, but over the years, your insurance consultant may be your most constant advisor. You may well outgrow your accountant and even your lawyer, but it is unlikely that you'll ever outgrow a good insurance consultant. It is hard to conceive of a business today that does not require highly competent insurance advice. Life, disability, health, fire and theft, liability, and business interruption insurance may seem like luxuries. But they are necessities.

You will need an honest, knowledgeable insurance advisor to help you decide which types of insurance are necessities and which are luxuries. The advisor must be able to tell you what kind of insurance you need, when you need it, and how you should pay for it. If you have a loss, he or she must tell you how to take proceeds.

Unfortunately, most insurance advisors are on commission. Their advice is, in fact, incidental to the "product" they sell. So it's especially important to select an insurance advisor with high integrity. Or you may consider arranging to pay for advice through upfront service fees instead of through commissions per policy. Some agents are starting to work that way.

It is important to develop a comprehensive relationship. It is a mistake to have one expert advise you on corporate insurance matters and another on your personal insurance needs. The insurance advisor's decisions will be more helpful if they result from a full knowledge of both your business and personal needs. Don't forget, this relationship should be entered into with the idea that it will be long term.

Lawyer.   Select a business lawyer who specializes in representing entrepreneurs. Ideally, find one who has helped clients start their businesses and worked with them through the full cycle to selling out, going public, or just getting big and successful, but who still enjoys helping new businesspeople.

You will be appalled at the cost of hiring a lawyer before there is any apparent need for one but planning ahead is a wise investment. Doing so will prove far less costly over time. If you have chosen the right lawyer, she or he will be invaluable to you in the business formation. Finally, select a lawyer who tells you how to do what you want to do.

Financial Consultants.   "I'm just starting out. Everything I have is being invested in the business, and all I earn must be plowed back there, too. The last thing I need is a financial or investment consultant." I have heard that message, over and over, from new entrepreneurs. And I always tell them they are wrong.

Money has a way of sneaking up on entrepreneurs, who are too busy to pay proper attention to their money. After all, that's why they don't want to spend time dealing with the selection of a consultant until they "need" one. Instead, I urge clients to choose a financial/investment consultant before they need one, so they can work together on personal and business financial goals and procedures to automate implementation before money is wasted.

In choosing a financial/investment consultant, find one who represents numerous other entrepreneurs who are or were just like you. A prestigious firm backing such a consultant ensures availability of information and advice beyond his or her expertise as well as a deep pocket for recourse should you receive negligent or fraudulent advice.

Special Consultants. No matter what business you're in, you'll soon discover there are consultants to it. Besides consultants in areas that transcend industries, such as consultants on the environment, personnel, computer systems, and quality control, there are ultra-specific niche consultants such as fitting room operation consultants for clothing stores, scent experts for the perfume and cosmetics businesses, and orthopedic surgeons for exercise equipment manufacturers. Although such consultants may seem expensive, they can be a lot cheaper than full-time, in-house staff and can lend credibility to your new business.

Guidelines for Choosing Professional Help

If you can, seek out professionals who will be able to fulfill present and future needs. But be realistic. As you start out, you may not be able to attract a professional of that stature. In that case, pick for the present and change later.

In addition to the particular services you expect from professionals, they may help you find and attract good directors, executives, other professionals, advisors, suppliers, financiers, bankers, and even customers. Gauging that capability and a willingness to help with it should be an important factor in your quest.

Once you have hired one satisfactory professional, ask that professional to refer you to other good professionals. If you have an accountant on board, ask that person to refer you to a lawyer and/or an insurance consultant. It is your responsibility, though, to carefully qualify that referral. Some professionals feel they must refer clients to certain professionals who refer clients to them, in the spirit of reciprocity. The integrity of the referring professional is critical. (Don't confuse good service or even results with integrity.)

Network.   For example, ask your banker for the name of a client who began as you did—one with similar goals or a personality not unlike yours. Find out if he or she has had the same lawyer or accountant for a long period.

Beware the False Positive.   When you network with friends and other entrepreneurs, be aware that many people say they have the best professional possible. But they may be uncritical or may not have the same needs that you do. *Beware the false negative,* as well. Some businesspeople prefer not to share good people. Others simply don't want to be responsible if anything goes wrong—even though the professional in question has never let them down.

Cross-Check.   If your accountant refers you to a new lawyer, ask your banker about the lawyer. Don't just ask whether that lawyer is good; make the banker be specific as to why he or she thinks the lawyer would be good for you.

Interview Your Prospects.   Interviews are free, after all. Be sure to prepare carefully for the interview. Know your needs and know what questions will help you determine whether a particular candidate is the professional you are seeking.

These interviews are often called "beauty contests." Don't treat them that superficially. You want more than a "pretty face" or congeniality. Ask how they deal, day to day, with existing clients. Take notes; that tends to keep the speaker more honest.

Interview the team, not just the team leader. Be sure you interview the minder (the professional who handles clients' matters), not just the finder (the salesperson who brings the clients in). Some professionals both find and mind; that's okay. They need not be a grinder (the professional who does the day-to-day grunt work). That's okay—as long as grinders are available to the minder.

Ask the candidate for references. Confidentiality may prevent professionals from giving names without client permission. But you can ask the candidate to get consent from several clients. If the candidate can't set up this arrangement with her or his clients, then something is clearly wrong. Find someone else.

Persuading Top Professionals to Work for You

Remember that top pros are busy. They can give just so many hours of personal service per week. The best ones will have to be convinced that both you and your dream have potential.

Understand Their Needs and Goals. Most good professionals aren't in it only for the fees, just as you, as an entrepreneur, aren't in it solely for the money. They generally want clients who will foster long-term relationships. (It takes time and costs money to create new relationships.) They want clients who listen. It is very frustrating to work for clients who never listen. But they should listen to you, too. The professional wants assurance that, as you grow your business, you will stay on board, so pick one with the capacity to serve long term. Professionals also want clients who will bring them new business. Let them know you have a network. Act confident. Professionals want winners for clients that will boost their business reputation.

Coordinate a Team. Use your professionals wisely by coordinating them to work as a team. You should decide which professional has the insight and leadership to quarterback all matters that require multiple disciplines. It may make sense to rotate that function, matching skills to different projects.

Professionals may need a quarterback in-house to coordinate multiple matters handled by one firm, a lawyer who handles your real estate and another who does your contracts. Talk to members of each discipline to determine whether each of the firms can assume that responsibility internally, without leading to inordinate costs.

Use Their Business Insights. Some professionals have considerable depth of experience. If you have one or more professionals with this attribute, count yourself lucky. If that extra dimension, that valuable business insight, exists, don't lose it, use it!

Brainstorming. From time to time, do some brainstorming with your team of professionals. This may cost more but it can prove invaluable. This can improve your substantive advice. A network can result that will lead to other resources.

Your Professional as Partner.   Professionals sometimes make good partners. But before you take this particular plunge, be sure to evaluate your needs within this context. If the professional becomes your partner, can he or she continue to serve you effectively? Conflicts of interest may arise. Ask yourself whether a piece of the action is necessary to buy the professional's attention. Is the professional so preoccupied with getting a piece of the action that she or he won't serve you if you refuse to come through? Each situation is different; understand yours and think it through carefully.

14
Drive and Energy

Beware of rashness, but with energy and sleep-less vigilance go forward and give us victories.
ABRAHAM LINCOLN

Most successful entrepreneurs have above-average physical energy and stamina. Given the nature of their origins, they must. When they strike out on their own, they take on their boss's job as well as their own job. Having two jobs does require excess energy and stamina. In addition, most entrepreneurs who start a business from scratch have less capital and staff than they need. No longer are there the colleagues down the hall to answer questions or brainstorm with or the assistants to help with all the things involved in running a business. Inevitably, there are chores which will remain undone if the founder doesn't do them.

Many of the entrepreneurs I've represented and interviewed talk about their willingness to do even the most menial tasks. That behavior is not just a reluctance to delegate or a fear of surrendering control. They also cherish their baby. They are proud of what they've created and believe the creation reflects on them. They all do whatever it takes and don't think much of their doing it. The extra effort comes with the territory. Although this effort consumes physical energy and stamina, entrepreneurs don't mind. They paraphrase the Boys Town poster: "He ain't heavy, he's my baby." They do it in interesting ways.

Entrepreneurs frequently find themselves doing so much that the time available for sleep is dramatically diminished. Some entrepreneurs told me they get a "full night's sleep." By probing, I discovered that most had slept far less during the earlier stages of their business; some never reduced their allotted time for sleep.

If, as an entrepreneur, you can't do much about your quantity of sleep—either because of the necessary moonlighting or the restricted budget and infrastructure—then at least consider dealing with the quality of your sleep. You can learn to improve.

Sleep, for most of us, occurs in patterns resembling an inverted bell curve (picture the silhouette of the Liberty Bell turned upside down). At the beginning and end of our sleep period—as we fall asleep and as we wake up—our sleep is shallow. That is when we experience creative dreams. Deep sleep, pictured at the longest vertical point of the bell, is when we replenish our energy and stamina. Entrepreneurs can live with less shallow sleep, because their focus lets them do their dreaming while awake and often while doing other things, but their deep sleep is critical to refuel their energy reserves.

Einstein was known to sleep a lot, but Edison got very little. Einstein's forte was deep thinking, perhaps best accomplished in the uninterrupted phases of shallow sleep. Edison, on the other hand, was a doer, a tinkerer, and needed to be awake more, in case a light bulb went on over his head.

Teach yourself to fall in and out of your deep sleep phase as rapidly as possible, so you can sleep less while still getting all the deep sleep you need. I taught myself to do that many years ago, and I have never regretted it. By getting only four hours of sleep, I had ample time to found my law firm and assist clients in starting their businesses. I can get more sleep when needed and get by on less when circumstances dictate.

Paul Loeb suddenly realized that the whole world was sleeping when it came to trucking. He developed a concept that kept him awake longer than most.

Profile

Paul Loeb's Sandlot Economics:
The Deadhead Route to Profit

You should be so lucky. Paul Loeb's idea was so obvious and so lucrative he could hardly believe his good fortune. Paul's father was in a commodity business. He and a dozen rivals supplied high-quality "silica" sand to the glass industry.

It was a boring business. Paul tried his hand at it and got lucky. He landed a couple of major contracts with giant corporations because he happened to call on these prospects on his father's behalf when both were dissatisfied with their suppliers. But Paul was more interested in his uncle's business. His uncle was a commodity trader.

He thought that traders were savvy, quick-witted entrepreneurs. Just the ticket for a savvy, quick-witted young man like Paul Loeb. But while Paul was thinking about joining his uncle, he chatted with a next-door neighbor whose father owned a top home furnishings company. The neighbor managed the company's trucking operation that delivered the merchandise for his father to Mendota, Illinois, not far from where Paul's father picked up sand. Paul learned that the home furnishing trucks came back empty—deadheading, as they call it. How about filling the trucks with sand on the way back?

"That would be no problem. I could offset my cost," the neighbor said. Paul said,

> "I will give you $200 a truck load," just taking the figure off the top of my head. Well, the going rate was $450, so I gave him $200. We ended up charging the sand companies $350, saving them $100, and I was pocketing $150. I said this is too easy. I found one or two other private fleets that were delivering products and going back empty. A great opportunity. So I severed ties with my dad, took $3000, opened a checking account and had a 100 square foot office and a rotary phone.

As simple as that, Paul was in business. No one begrudged him his profits, because all his customers were saving big bucks on transportation. As he told me, "I was making so much money, so fast, that I figured this had to come to an end, that there was something wrong. And there was something wrong. This was a totally regulated industry when I started this, so we shouldn't have been doing this."

Paul was 24 when the business was deregulated. He was well-known in the trade as a savvy young man who was reliable and who got things done. It was easy for him to capitalize in the new free environment and build a major business.

It was simple, yes. But it wasn't easy. Paul spent long days in that 10-by-10-foot office, about as big as a small bedroom. He was very busy. For an entire year, he did it all "all by myself. I carried my typewriter home at night and typed the invoices. I did all my own collections. I worked 20 hours a day."

With deregulation, Paul Loeb began to expand a lot. Soon he had many coworkers. Their support enabled Paul to "get a life." He married and had a family and was able to work more normal hours.

Here's how to learn to get by with less sleep:

1. *Learn self-hypnosis.* Buy a book on hypnosis. Even if you are afraid of being hypnotized by someone else, there is nothing to fear in self-hypnosis; your free will is preserved. Eventually, your powers of suggestion—actually your mind's susceptibility to your own suggestion—will become so keen that the suggestion of deep sleep will work instantly. Don't worry about waking up. By suggesting to yourself that you get out of bed when the alarm rings and by setting the alarm earlier, you will come out of your deep sleep without lingering in the shallow phase. Don't worry, even if the alarm fails, you'll surely awaken, actually quite well rested.

    If you don't perfect the self-hypnosis system, you still will have improved your sleeping style. You may not eliminate the phase-in and phase-out stages, but you will shorten them. That alone makes the exercise worthwhile, and with time, you will continue to improve your technique.

2. *Buy a reliable alarm clock and obey it.* Get a good alarm clock and you'll be confident that sleeping deep will not cause you

to oversleep. Then, the crutch of shallow sleep won't be necessary. Be sure to get in the habit of getting up when the clock rings, otherwise the crutch will be unreliable, and you will be reluctant to fall into a deep sleep.

3. *Understand what you can't do in your sleep.* Most entrepreneurial dreams occur, and all of them get implemented, while the entrepreneur is awake. It stands to reason that the more you are awake (within reason), the better your chance of having a dream and converting it to reality. Knowing that should cause you to use your entrepreneurial passion to make you achieve a somnambulist stage quickly.

4. *Take care of yourself.* Let your physician know about your sleep program and get his or her advice on vitamins, a balanced diet, and an exercise regimen.

5. *Listen to your body.* This deep sleep technique isn't a perfect science. You may underestimate or overindulge. Too much of a good thing can still be too much. If your body is too tired, use the same self-hypnosis technique to take a nap or a catnap. When I get on a plane, I often nap before leaving the gate. Then I'm full of energy to work during the flight.

Go with the Flow

The first lesson to learn about energy is don't fight it, harness it. Have you ever paddled a canoe down stream? The secret is to use the river's currents, not fight them. You should control your direction and keep your balance, but remember that the best forward momentum is left to the natural current.

People who are driven, who feel they must be doing everything, find it difficult to accept that some things are best done by other forces. This is difficult for entrepreneurs to understand because they are intent on being in the driver's seat. When you drive your car, you use some of your energy to steer, but you rely on gasoline for the energy to make the car go. Similarly, as an entrepreneur, you can be in control and use other energy that can help reach your destination. It shouldn't matter to entrepreneurs whether they row their dream each stroke of the way to reality or they harness a new energy source by using an existing flow to carry them there. The latter has the added benefit of freeing the entrepreneur to improve the voyage in other ways, and that is clearly preferable.

Work Your Heart Out

Time just doesn't seem to be the critical test. Margie Korshak said, "My work ethic is 24 hours a day if that is what it takes." But, later, she admitted that some days she works 18 hours and other days 4 hours. More and more, I have come to believe that the quality, not the quantity, of effort is what distinguishes entrepreneurs from other businesspeople. Margie Korshak talked about what she was willing to do, saying, "I'm not so fancy. If I have to stuff an envelope here, I stuff an envelope. Whatever it takes to get the job done."

The requisite quality of an entrepreneur's work ethic is not just hard work. Thurman Rodgers said it best, "I'm a tough, smart guy and I work my ass off. But in our industry, there are a lot of tough, smart guys who work real hard. I realize I have to earn my way in; that's my responsibility." Recognizing that responsibility to earn your way to success is a key component of the entrepreneurial work ethic.

Eileen Ford, who has created so many successful, famous models, advises you, as a would-be entrepreneur: "Don't just wait for success to come from the tooth fairy because there is no tooth fairy. To be really successful, you have to work your heart out; time can't mean anything to you."

Although Ford refers to "time," her concept transcends time. "Work your heart out" is an interesting phrase, especially coming from someone who told me that she loves to work and that the opposite of work is death. I like her phrase because it highlights the need for the effort to come from your heart.

It's not how much you work or how hard you work or how you think about working, but how you feel about working. "Work your heart out" means indulging in something because of a passion; workaholism, on the other hand, means escaping from something because passion is lacking.

For Sheila Cluff, paying her dues has nothing to do with how much she does; her dues are measured by what she doesn't do. Sheila, the founder of Sheila's Spas in California, escaped into a business catering to customers trying to escape from their work. She says, matter-of-factly, "There are those 12- to 14-hour days and seven-day weeks. Sometimes you feel resentful over the many things other people are doing that are a great deal of fun, that I couldn't do because I had decided on a particular road. You have to make sacrifices. You have to give up something. I don't believe you can 'have it all.'"

Hard work and sacrifice may have been somewhat easier for Sheila because her parents were role models. Her mother worked as a chemist during the day and, at night, joined Sheila's father at the little service station he founded. "It just didn't occur to me," Sheila says, "that people didn't work seven-day weeks and that you didn't work all day and then do the paper work at night on the dining room table."

Because of her upbringing, paying her dues may seem easier for Sheila than for others, but it is not. Sheila has a family. Her husband and children are understanding and supportive (the family had pulled up stakes and moved to California to accommodate Sheila's dream), but demands still exist. How can she fit all her responsibilities in and still have a social life? Sheila solved her problem by adjusting her needs to her priorities. She decided to combine socializing with her desire to be with her family, so she rejects any social invitations that do not include her family. No doubt, those invitations that fail to include family and are rejected eventually stop coming. The dues are high. But Sheila has prioritized her commitments to accommodate her primary goal—making her dream real.

To become entrepreneurial, you must work your heart out. That may well entail hard work, long hours, and major sacrifice. But you must follow your heart, so it can cause you to work as much as you need to pull off your dream. That's what I mean by paying your dues.

15

Entrepreneurs Are Leaders

There is nothing as invigorating as the ego boost that comes from having others—some of them virtual strangers—sign on when your company is just a dream. What they are saying when they agree to service customers, suppliers, employers or distributors is that they believe in you. They may never express that as unambiguously again.

JOSHUA HYATT
"Mapping the Entrepreneurial Mind," *Inc.,*
August 1991

Entrepreneurs are leaders. That's not a mere coincidence; being a leader is a prerequisite to entrepreneurship! Even if you are the only employee in your business, you still must be a leader, to attract, retain, and get the most out of suppliers, financiers, customers, professionals, consultants, and other independent contractors, and maybe even yourself. For a business to move in the right direction—toward accomplishment of the key goals— someone must lead the way. Once you remove your boss as your leader, the logical successor is you. Of course, some entrepreneurs are better than others; some have more opportunities than others to show what they are made of; some lead in ways which are easy to observe and understand, while others' ways are less visible or comprehensible; but they are all leaders.

If you're like most people, when you find out that all entrepreneurs are leaders, you'll think that precludes you from joining their ranks. Because you weren't president or captain of anything in school, you think that you aren't a leader. Yet, although Sam Walton was president of his student council, most entrepreneurs never held an office of any kind. A few were school team captains and community or social club presidents, but most were managers, a difference you'll soon understand.

In his book, *On Becoming a Leader,* Warren Bennis, an authority on leadership, says: "I think there's been a peculiar idolatry of leaders." He's right; we are accustomed to leaders being bigger than life. They are the names that describe history: Attila, Caesar, Bonaparte, Washington, Lincoln, Lenin, Roosevelt, Hitler, Churchill, Stalin, Eisenhower, Mao, Ghandi, and King. Not all leaders are recorded in history, but then not all leaders change the world. Some barely change their own lives. Entrepreneurs, however, do change things, certainly the nerve structure of their own business and often their own lives.

Independence and control are the principal motivating factors for people who become their own bosses. Entrepreneurs no longer want to be led by someone else—their boss. They want to lead and be their own boss and maybe boss some others. But can *you* do that? After all, you're no Julius Caesar, Napoleon Bonaparte, or Dwight Eisenhower.

You may think those leaders were born with their leadership talent. Some small elements of leadership may come with birth, but those elements tend to determine the quality of the leadership, not the existence of leadership talent. For example, intellect can improve the quality of leadership—as well as the quality of many other roles—but it doesn't automatically make one a leader. Parental training and education may affect leadership skills, but these influences encourage experimentation rather than offering motivation or lessons on how to be a leader. Many people don't learn how to be leaders during school days. The opportunity usually arises later, and for you, that later can be now.

Very few entrepreneurs are quite like the historic leaders we admire. If they had been like them, few would have become entrepreneurs. So, it doesn't matter that you are not Douglas MacArthur, because that wouldn't make you entrepreneurial anyway. What is important is that you can learn sufficient leadership traits to pursue your entrepreneurial dream. The teaching is easy and so is the learning, as you will see.

The goal of this chapter is not to teach you to lead the world, the nation, an army, or even a large corporation. Its lesson is limited to teaching you to lead only those you need to lead in order to become an entrepreneur. Once you are an entrepreneur, you may want or need more and different training to expand your leadership capability and to keep up with your growing business. It's a lot like learning to swim. This chapter will teach you how to get in the water and cross the pool, but you'll need more lessons before you swim the English Channel.

What Is a Leader?

Get rid of the image you have in your mind: The general on his horse, waving his sword and shouting orders to his troops. At best, that general is only one kind of leader. Many generals are mere managers, and many of those who are leaders are implementing the goals and dreams of others.

People often say "He acts like a leader," "You'll know a leader when you see one," or "She has leadership potential." Those sayings might lead you to believe that there is a generally accepted profile of a leader. There is not. Leaders come in all sizes, shapes, persuasions, and nationalities. Some lead toward good; others toward evil. Their styles are as varied as their distinct personalities. Patton and Eisenhower, Lenin and King, Washington and Ghandi, Hitler and Lincoln: Each pair is a striking example of how leaders can vary as to goal, style, and image.

Leaders may differ, yet you recognize that every one of the people I've cited was a leader. You can judge people's ability to lead by the results they achieve. Leaders are heroes or villains because of their accomplishments. We almost always spot leaders by witnessing their accomplishments; then we trace back to their efforts to understand what enabled them to lead.

Harold Geneen viewed his job as "making other people succeed," and says "leadership is convincing people to do what you want because it will help them." Of course, he assumes that the leader is "on the level with them, as well as objective, fair and loyal to his followers' interests." Following from that premise is his belief that a leader is one who can demonstrate that he or she is strong enough to carry the follower and is willing to help.

There is a lot of literature on leadership. Each author has his or her own criteria, but the most commonly cited characteristics include:

1. A realistic but clear vision of a goal, the means to accomplish it, and a sense of how, once achieved, success will be measured and rewarded; and

2. the ability to communicate the vision, the means, and the measure to others, so that they are inspired to believe that the goal is worth achieving, that it is achievable by that leader, and that they will be rewarded for helping the process.

Leaders Aren't Managers

To understand what a leader is—for managers tend to look somewhat like leaders—you must know the difference between leaders and managers. A few people, of course, are both, but many managers are devoid of leadership talent, and many leaders lack management talent. Understanding the difference helps to clarify what a leader is.

Remember how entrepreneurs and managers handle risks differently? Managers kept both personal computers (the risk PC and the reward PC) in front of them forever, whereas entrepreneurs put the risk PC behind them quickly so that they can get on toward the rewards. Leaders and managers compare in a similar manner to entrepreneurs and managers. Leaders can create a positive-sum game, whereas managers tend to deal in a zero-sum game. Managers take the existing universe (market, personnel talent pool, capital resources) and concentrate on increasing their share, which reduces someone else's share. Leaders create new shares, by expanding the universe, by generating new talent, new markets, and new capital sources. Managers instruct people on what to do, but leaders help them decide what they want to do. These are some guidelines for understanding and describing the difference. There are other criteria too.

Professors Nanus and Bennis, in *On Becoming a Leader,* make a most interesting distinction between managers and leaders:

Managers do things right.

Leaders do the right thing.

Notice that Nanus and Bennis don't say that leaders do the good thing (plenty of leaders have evil goals) but, instead, the right thing. To leaders, the goal is what matters; to managers, the means are the key. Leaders do what seems correct to the audience of potential followers whom they aim to attract. Some leaders select their action in order to attract followers. Others just do what seems right and the followers seem to find them.

Before becoming the consummate venture capitalist, Dan Tolkowsky had another profession. After graduation from the Imperial College in London, Tolkowsky was a pilot in the Royal Air Force, later moving to Israel, and, ultimately, commanding the highly regarded Israeli Air Force. An accomplished military and business leader as well as a student of leadership, Tolkowsky uses levels of military leadership to distinguish entrepreneurial leadership from management:

In the army, a battalion commander knows exactly what is before him and what he is supposed to do with the enemy facing him. He isn't the guy who will make up his mind to go to Berlin.

In business, the guy who spies out the land, sees the opportunity and says "On to Berlin" is an entrepreneur. He's got to be able to think strategically and tactically.

Others say management is tactics and leadership is strategy. A World War II story about a supposed solution to the German U-boats illustrates the difference between strategy and tactics. A British Admiral proposed heating up the Atlantic until it boiled, which would explode all the U-boats. An American admiral said, "That's great, but how do you get the Atlantic to boil?"

"That," said the Brit, "is tactics; I'm involved only in strategy." At least one admiral would disagree. Admiral Grace Hopper, the first woman to achieve the rank of admiral in the U.S. Navy, thinks the difference between managing and leading relates more to whether you focus on ideas or people, rather than whether you are involved in strategy or tactics. She said "You don't manage people, you manage things. You lead people."

I remember a lecture by Nobel Laureate Elie Weisel, where he uttered one of the wisest and most broadly applicable sayings: "Questions are what bring us together; answers are what drive us apart." Leaders *ask* their followers to join them in reaching a goal; managers tell them the *answer*—how to solve a problem—and then tell them to use that solution.

Both managers and leaders encourage, motivate, and help their followers. Leaders tend to create an atmosphere that converts the optional to the imperative and the improbable to the likely. In most of life, the risk-reward ratio is incomplete. Even if you know all the risks and all the rewards, you probably don't know the likelihood of any or all of them occurring. Managers can help you fill in the list of risks and rewards; good managers can help you analyze both sides and the balance. Leaders cause the scale to tip by making the rewards seem more certain and more desirable.

Have you heard of the Peter Principle? That's the theory that says people are promoted beyond their capabilities. For example, the best salesperson may be elevated to sales manager, even though she knows nothing about managing. As a result, the company gets a bad manager and loses a good salesperson. Situations like that happen frequently. A leader is not necessarily the one who is best at doing what must get done. He or she is, instead, the one who can motivate others to believe they can, with effort, become the best at whatever they do.

Terminating Employees

Some of the most unpleasant episodes in your life as a compassionate human being are those moments when you must tell employees they are being terminated. You are, in effect, telling someone in the most dramatic manner possible that he or she does not measure up to the requirements of the job in your organization.

You may be sending a worse message, one that may be all too true. You may, in effect, be branding someone an incompetent in his or her chosen profession. Nothing can be more devastating to the human spirit than this.

Be Fair. Once you have decided to pursue this course, be sure that you have done all that you can do—or should have done—before the moment arrives. As early as possible, communicate your expectations; keep the employee posted when he or she begins falling short of expectations. You must also be sure that the fault lies with the employee and not with yourself or a manager.

Be Compassionate. A pink slip is a most inappropriate Christmas gift but an all-too-common stocking stuffer. At the end of the year, entrepreneurs, like their counterparts in corporations, start looking for ways to dress up the annual profit and loss statement. Don't give an employee the axe for a birthday present, either. You have birthday information on file. You should be mindful of employee anniversaries, too.

Try to let the employee save face, especially when the cost is inconsequential. It is invariably better to allow an employee to resign. But if this becomes a habit, you will get a reputation as a bad employer, probably deserved. It suggests that you don't know how to pick people or you don't know what to expect and how to get it.

Whatever you do, save those words of indignation for the privacy of a sound-proof office, and remember that voices travel further when saying negative things, so keep your volume down. Otherwise, your notice that the employee resigned will have a hollow ring. Also, if overheard, the reprimand can throw a pall over an office, lower company morale, and reduce productivity. And use restraint. There is no need to destroy an employee's dignity. To do so endangers your own. It also puts you at risk of litigation (harassment), wrongful discharge, and slander. And, in this society, it may put you, your other employees, or your family at risk of physical danger.

Protect Yourself.   These are litigious—even dangerous—times. Fill the unsatisfactory employee's file with memos—yours or the employee's supervisor's. The memos must document the reasons for firing. Be specific. Item: "John Johnson was absent today but didn't call in. I called, and he said he was ill. He said he meant to call in but was so groggy he simply fell back to sleep. This is the third such instance. John was to attend an important lunch meeting with our key client."

When you actually fire the employee, try to have one witness present, such as the immediate supervisor, unless overwhelming circumstances make absolute privacy essential. It is best to fire at the end of the day, when peers are gone, even if this means doing it after a midnight shift is completed. Don't forget to collect the employee's key, building pass, and corporate credit card. Do not be naive to the real risk of physical danger in certain situations. Know your employee. If he or she is troubled, be sure that you have adequate security measures in place.

Short and sweet beats a vintage whine. You may delay the dread day because you want to be a nice person. But delay sends the wrong message. It is confusing to the employee on the way out and to the employees who will be staying.

In these litigious times, employees often seek revenge through false claims of discrimination and/or sexual harassment. This is especially true of employees who cannot cope with personal shortcomings. The more careful and methodical you are in laying the foundation, the earlier the firing process, the better the result. Proper treatment of terminated employees not only avoids enemies and protects against spurious claims, it also shows your sense of fairness to remaining employees. This sense does more for morale and loyalty than the holiday party and picnic combined.

By Whom the Bell Tolls.   Many entrepreneurs believe in the little sign Harry Truman posted on his desk in the Oval Office, "The buck stops here." These people will do their own firing. Others feel that cluttering their minds with employee relations is undesirable. Firing is just one of those delegated responsibilities. Those who feel that way will pass off this unenviable task to subordinates. The key is to be mindful of chains of command and of the morale of the remaining workers. Weigh those factors when you decide which supervisors should fire which employees.

Who Should Be Fired.   Entrepreneurs may learn from their own mistakes, but they also rationalize them. Entrepreneurs tend to believe that it is the project that failed and not themselves. That's fine. But the attitude becomes unhealthy—counterproductive—if the entrepreneur becomes hypocritical, demanding 100 percent perfection from employees while tolerating far less from himself or herself. Managers who train employees well and who give proper latitude of responsibility and authority encounter more employee mistakes—at least initially. But as time wears on and the concept wears in, well-trained employees will reward the entrepreneur with better overall results.

The Firing Line.   The key to doing this unpleasant chore well is to determine the point at which retaining the employee is no longer fair—to you, to the employee, to the other employees, to suppliers, and to customers. To paraphrase George Orwell again, remember that all mistakes are not equal. Distinguish between those that can be and are corrected and those that recur, those that teach no lessons and so indicate bigger problems—such as a lack of capability, and, the cardinal sin, a lack of caring.

Are Leaders Good Followers?

When I was a kid, I remember teachers telling the class that if we wanted to become good leaders, we first had to learn to be good followers. I didn't buy it then, and I don't buy it now. It's important for leaders to understand the needs and motivations of their followers, but they don't have to become followers to do so. Followers seek to shift responsibility for their lives to others. For them, it is easier to function if responsibility for whatever might go wrong can be blamed on someone else (for example, their boss) rather than on themselves. They surrender independence, self-determination, and control willingly, in order to avoid blame. Leaders, on the other hand, gladly accept responsibility for themselves, as well as for those they lead.

Bob Engelman is an entrepreneurial leader who founded one successful savings and loan company and subsequently led the merger of another with an insurance company, creating a financial services company dramatically different than its predecessors. He was once a manager—a high-, but not the highest, ranking officer at a successful regional bank. One of the reasons Bob left the bank was that the bank's atmosphere stifled his ability to lead. Interestingly, Bob did not feel stifled by the managers who served above him but by his commitment to those below him. His responsibilities to them and the attendant time commitment prevented him from doing what he wanted, proving how important it is to have the right followers in the appropriate atmosphere.

Bob had good entrepreneurial characteristics; he is an excellent leader. However, Bob wasn't able to break from his long-time employer and become an entrepreneur until he realized that his need to lead was even greater than his desire not to follow.

Entrepreneurial Leaders

Leading without a boss is different from leading with a boss. Without a boss, you must devise your own goals and plans, supply your own dreams and procedures, bear the ultimate responsibility, and determine how rewards are shared. When you have a boss, his or her dreams and goals are your map.

Entrepreneurs start in a vacuum, which their dream is meant to fill. Nonentrepreneurs—even those who are leaders—arrive after the vacuum has been abhorred and filled. First, having no existing organization or system, entrepreneurs proceed without a boss. Second, for the same reason, they start without any followers—the religious leaders have those of their persuasions; the political leaders have the members of their parties or the residents in their precincts; and the military leaders have their recruits and lower ranking officers. All those other leaders must do is lead. Entrepreneurial leaders must also create and attract their followers before they can lead them.

You've seen great entrepreneurs. They believe in their dreams so strongly that you wonder about your wisdom, even your sanity, if you doubt them. They may seem brash or offensive to some, but they never seem that way to those who believe them. Their followers don't just *believe them,* they also *believe in them.* They are not just good at selling; they are what they are selling. When my clients are considering an investment in a start-up business, I always warn them that, in this case, "the three most important things are people, people, people." That's my way of helping my clients remember that what they are buying is the entrepreneur who is selling them.

How do entrepreneurs create and attract their followers? They are not just cheerleaders, they are troubadours singing the praises of their dreams. Believing in your dream is not enough. You must be willing to proclaim publicly your belief and risk the embarrassment of being wrong. If you believe wholeheartedly and, if you demonstrate that to others, followers will be attracted to the dream and the dreamer.

Have you ever watched a couple who have a great marriage or parents who have a "perfect" relationship with their child? You wish you could achieve that relationship, so you emulate it. Well, the same is true of those who observe an entrepreneur who is fully committed to a dream. The difference is that an observer cannot become part of someone else's marriage or family but can "buy into" an entrepreneur's project. They buy in with investment, employment, independent contracting, supplying, or purchasing, because they too believe in the entrepreneur's dream, as well as the ability of the entrepreneur to make it real.

For some, the image of an entrepreneurial leader is one of a tyrant, who gives orders, doles out drudge chores, shares few profits, and selects subordinates who are not achievers. In times past, such behavior was more prevalent, but so was slavery. Thankfully, both seem to be passé. Although there are exceptions, most entrepreneurs, today, lead by different means.

Pat Ryan, a consummate leader initially, built Aon Insurance by acquiring old-line companies whose assets and profits were greater than his. Those companies were owned by men such as W. Clement Stone, General (Ret.) John Brogan, and the late John O'Brien, the entrepreneurs who founded them, and were well established and profitable. Pat was a virtual upstart—an unranked rookie taking on champs. Pat had to convince them that his dream was better than theirs or they never would have surrendered their "babies"—no matter what the price. I know, because I represented John Brogan and John O'Brien when they sold Youngberg Carlson, a well-established, profitable insurance agency, to that upstart named Pat Ryan. Stone, Brogan, and O'Brien were all entrepreneurial leaders. To sell out to Ryan meant they had to respect his entrepreneurial leadership abilities.

I asked Pat Ryan, some 15 years later, to describe the leadership skills that enabled him to succeed. Pat says that people want to associate with a leader who will provide them with a positive experience. That necessitates insight, technical ability, and integrity—to ensure that dreams are reasonable, achievement is feasible, and rewards will be fair. It also requires the ability to communicate the pragmatics, the "rightness," the commitment, and the magic.

Pat feels he succeeded in attracting his followers by explaining clearly to them what he was about, what his goals and principles were, and how he would run the business. Once they believed that he had an achievable mission and that he had a sense of fairness, they were Pat's to lead.

Stef Wertheimer is another entrepreneur who has shunned the old ways of dealing with followers. Stef was ten in 1937, when his family fled from Germany to Israel. Lacking fluency in Hebrew, he did poorly in school and had to become an apprentice. Using what he learned working with the British during World War II, he joined the underground in Israel. After serving as an officer in Israel's War of Independence, he decided that the military and government were not where he wanted to work. He wanted to be his own boss and "not be employed by anyone else." So, he started his own business, Iscar, a manufacturer of cutting tools, which today employs two thousand people and corners nearly 10 percent of the world's market.

Although Iscar's accomplishments can be determined by the bottom line, Stef's require further analysis, for he is a unique leader as entrepreneurs go. Stef grew up in Israel at a time when the kibbutz was the predominant socioeconomic unit. A kibbutz is a socialistic community where residents work for the common good, with all compensation and assets inuring to the group account from which the needs of each are satisfied. Stef adopted some of the kibbutz mentality, and his progressive approach to labor relations has become well known. But Stef is a capitalist, which generally is not perceived as compatible with socialism. He refers to his approach as a "capitalistic kibbutz system," combining the profit motive with social responsibility.

George Kalidonis, president of Technology Planning and Development Corp. and managing general partner of Chicago Capital Fund, refers to David McClelland, a Harvard psychologist whose research focused on successful entrepreneurs in India, Malawi, and Ecuador. One of the important personal characteristics McClelland found was a commitment to others, sacrificing short-term gain for long-term goodwill, a creed that is consistent with that of Pat Ryan and Stef Wertheimer.

That sacrifice seems at odds with venture capitalists' insistence on strong "internal rates of return," a measure of both how much money they get and how soon they get it out. Although the short-term goals of venture capitalists must be *served* by the entrepreneur, in order to attract capital, they need not be *embraced* as her or his own primary goal. Otherwise, they dissuade followers from making the often necessary sacrifices. And why should they sacrifice if it only benefits the venture capitalists?

Elmer Winter started Manpower from scratch. There were no temporary employment agencies for offices; that was the brilliant brainchild of Elmer and his partner. Their program for expansion to additional states, and eventually worldwide, and their concept of franchising local offices were ingenious. Their hard work and commitment were exceeded only by their risk.

When the time came for Manpower to go public, Elmer could have easily justified his value and accepted all the rewards accorded him through long and hard negotiations with the underwriters. After all, it was his idea, his risk, his long hours, and his sweat that made Manpower an international giant. Instead, after he got all he could from the underwriters, Elmer arranged to give some of his stock to the Manpower employees. He had absolutely no obligation to do so. Every employee got at least a share, and the stock they got was from Elmer, not from the company, the public shareholders, or the investment bankers.

Elmer recognized the contribution of all those who worked for Manpower and made it successful. He realized that his stock grant to employees would lower his IRR. But for Elmer, as for Pat and Stef, the commitment to which McClelland referred was paramount, and the short-term gain was readily sacrificed to achieve long-term goals. Regardless whether you agree that Elmer Winter is a leader, there can't be any doubt, after his stock grant, that his employees were ready to follow him anywhere.

Likewise, the entrepreneur who prematurely drains the business to support a personal lifestyle or who gears for an early bail-out sends signals to followers that their reward—compensation, purchase orders, fees, or friendly source of supply—may be too short-lived to justify loyalty. Joe Sullivan's advice, that entrepreneurs not assume obligations that will prevent them from seizing opportunities, must be expanded and extended, so they also don't establish excessive personal cash flow demands that require them to take short-term benefits from the business which would deplete their ability to lead.

Entrepreneurial leadership is too easily dissipated by personal excesses, considering how difficult it is to establish. How do you get entrepreneurial leadership? It isn't something you buy, whether with stock or cash. Where does it come from?

How Entrepreneurial Leadership Develops

Some people say that their entrepreneurial leadership just popped up suddenly. I asked Jim Covert, the entrepreneur behind SecurityLink, a commercial and residential security system company, when he became a leader. He said, "One day I realized that people listened to me, that I have the ability to motivate people and get them to work three times harder for me than for anyone else."

Jim Covert first demonstrated his entrepreneurial leadership when he gave up his love—performing with the Shadows of the Night, a 1960s popular band that recorded big hits, such as "Gloria," and had three gold records—in order to become the band's business manager, a talent which even Jim admits was more suitable for him. His roles as an M.P. sergeant and with the

U.S. Secret Service, charged with protecting three presidents and high-ranking foreign officials, honed his leadership skills. But Jim didn't realize that his entrepreneurial leadership was simultaneously improving.

Jim may have suddenly realized that people listened to him, but his achievement didn't happen that day but through a series of experiences. A lifetime of events gave Jim Covert the opportunity to lead. He saw what was needed, he tried it, and it worked. There's an old saying, "Nothing succeeds like success." That may be true, but I assure you that *nothing motivates like success*. Each time Jim Covert had a little success and noticed a few people listening to him, he was encouraged to grab for another ring and try a little more leadership.

Steps to Develop Your Entrepreneurial Leadership

The following 23 steps can help you develop your entrepreneurial leadership skills:

1. *Keep perspective.* You aren't out to lead nations or armies. Even though you may dream that some day your business will become big and successful, begin at the beginning. Right now, all you have to lead is the creation or change of the nerve structure, and the odds are you can lead that effort.

2. *Know why you want to lead.* Ed Beauvois knew why he wanted to lead. Ed told me, "It wouldn't bother me to work for a large company that was not my own, but it's difficult to find one that you really believe in." Perhaps your reason for leading is to pursue the dream you really believe in.

3. *Identify your targets; know when to shoot.* You must identify not only your dream but the specific ways you will achieve it, and how you will measure your success and share its rewards. If all you can identify is your dream, it probably will remain just that.

One of the best ways to know whether you are ready to lead is to pretend you are the follower and someone else is the leader pitching you. What I'm really proposing is a form of method acting. As Constantin Stanislavsky, the creator of method acting, said, you don't have to be a murderer to portray one in a play. Similarly, you can portray a follower. If you (the follower) don't buy your (the leader's) pitch, fix the pitch and try again, but this time portray a different follower. Eventually, you'll get your leadership into shape so that even you will take you seriously and want to follow you.

4. *Be clear and fixed.* Your description of your goal must be clear. First, that ensures that you understand it. Second, if you can't explain your dream to others, how can they evaluate it and you?

It's hard to hit a moving target. Unless your targets are fixed, people will not believe that you can hit them—and they may be right.

5. *Observe when people listen to you.* When someone follows your lead on anything, no matter how insignificant the occasion may seem, notice why they followed. Was it what you said or how you said it? Was it the confidence and ability you had or was it the confidence and ability you portrayed?

Bob Galvin is the retired CEO and principal shareholder of Motorola. His father, Paul Galvin, founded Motorola, originally a manufacturer of radios and later a maker of TVs. But it was Bob Galvin who transformed Motorola, moved it out of those businesses and made it a preeminent force in electronics and telecommunications. Bob told me that his "father ailed a lot but pushed himself and seemed (to others) to be a healthy and energized man" who would achieve his dreams. Would people have followed Paul Galvin if they knew he was ill and if they doubted that he could overcome the ailments?

6. *Leverage your small successes.* Bob Galvin has "unqualified respect for business founders," because "they are the leverage people of our society." One way entrepreneurs use leverage to lead is by using small successes to motivate themselves and others in a big way. You must learn to do that.

No dream entails only one success. Many steps are involved in making a dream real. Taking each step is a separate success. Learn to subdivide your efforts into separate steps and to take pride and joy in achieving each step.

Later, you will learn to apply the same steps toward your entrepreneurial dream. Let's assume your dream is a chain of cookie stores. You haven't decided what kinds of cookies, what recipes or what locations, but you have decided on a great name (which you have protected with a trade name registration). We all know that a great name alone will not create a successful business. However, by talking about the name and how it will be a hit, people will want to be part of the process. They may share with you their thoughts on product or location, and you will leverage small success—the company name—to greater success.

7. *Be tough, not mean; use carrots, not sticks.* I asked Harold Geneen about his reputation as a mean boss. He said, "People say so, but I don't think so. I get a lot of letters from people who say it was the most interesting period of their lives." Harold Geneen would agree that he is demanding, though.

Richie Melman feels exactly the same. He can spot a misplaced piece of silverware at a table as he hurriedly walks through one of his restaurants, and his employees hear about it. Richie believes "discipline is not a punishment but a tool with which [his] team can win." Discipline can cause teams to win but can also be intimidating to those who don't believe they can live up to the "perfectionist" standards of the leader.

Some followers will always perceive "tough" as "mean." There is nothing you can do about them. Others you can teach the difference, and they, along with you, will succeed. Many of today's leaders are graduates of Geneen's tough "school of management."

Lead by carrots; leave the stick at home. Those who follow entrepreneurs do so for the special carrot, and they won't be influenced by the sticks that sometimes work for managers.

8. *Let them see you err.* To err is human. To admit and correct your own error is a first step toward leadership. Geneen called entrepreneurship "the privilege of making your own mistakes," cautioning the need to be right more than you are wrong. Jim Covert quoted his former boss: "A successful leader is right 51 percent of the time but is the first to know he made mistakes and fixes them before anybody else knows he made mistakes. People will always perceive you as a genius if you fix your own problems before they see them."

I think Jim's former boss is partially correct. Everyone knows you're human, so they expect you to err. If, however, you know how to fix your errors, you demonstrate that human errors won't stop you from succeeding. It doesn't matter if others see your errors. It only matters that others see you fix them.

9. *Show you are willing to pay the price.* Demonstrate your willingness to sacrifice to make your dream real. Jenny Craig's personal experience supports her advice to would-be entrepreneurs, "Show it's so important that you're willing to be less perfect at being a mother or a wife." It helps, if you have Jenny's stamina and can rise at 5 a.m., as she does, to be able to do more. You don't have to copy Jenny's wake-up habits, but you do have to demonstrate to your followers that you are willing to pay the price for your success.

Jenny Craig also said that she doesn't know anyone who became an entrepreneur with a part-time attitude. That's part of paying the price; full-time commitment is expected of leaders.

10. *Create positive-sum games.* People who play zero-sum games are managers. They use existing momentum to tilt the field so the ball rolls their way. But where momentum does not yet exist, you must demonstrate your ability to increase the sum, to create "something" from nothing, if people are to believe in your entrepreneurial leadership and follow you.

11. *Withstand temptations.* If you perform well at work, your boss may offer you a tempting opportunity. Don't turn it down. To do so could mean your job and might deprive you of valuable lessons and growth. At the same time, keep it in perspective and don't fall for the temptation of forgetting your long-term goal—your dream.

12. *Study your opportunities.* The best way to learn this is through retrospect. Look at the opportunities you missed and think about what you should have done. Don't regret and recriminate; learn from your experiences. Do the same with opportunities other people miss. Don't just think once about what should have been done. Think, rethink, and then think again. Keep a list of opportunities you missed, and next to each write the reason you missed it. Keep thinking about opportunities—why they weren't spotted, how they should have been

spotted, how the ring should have been made golden, and how you should have grabbed it.

13. *Select the right followers.* It may seem presumptuous to select your followers, especially before you have any. On the contrary, having the gall to select your followers will help you convince them you are likely to succeed.

I've asked many entrepreneurs what kinds of people they hire to help them realize their dream. They've found that hiring overqualified people for every spot is not the best approach. It depletes precious capital; also, it can lead to boredom, low confidence, lack of support, and a myriad of other counter-productive tendencies in your followers.

You must attract the right followers. To determine who are the right followers, be honest with yourself. Know what you expect of them; know who can do what you expect and need; know what they need from you; and know what you are able and willing to give them. Select people who can help you reach your goal and who will follow you.

14. *Take responsibility for their mistakes.* Debbi Fields tells her employees that they'll never be blamed for mistakes, so long as they don't hide them from her. In effect, she is saying that she'll bear responsibility for their mistakes; that's what entrepreneurial leaders must do.

15. *Select the birds you flock with.* Jim Covert said, "There's a stronger kinship among people who don't have the guts to fail publicly, who are not willing to be entrepreneurs, than among those who are." Sometimes that kinship is inviting. Restrain yourself and hold out for membership in the courageous fraternity or sorority of risk takers who are willing to fail publicly.

16. *Give.* Although an entrepreneurial leader starts out without followers, ultimately you do want followers; having them makes you a leader. Everything you can do to attract and motivate followers works to your benefit. Therefore, when you give them hope by supporting them, it doesn't deplete your assets, it enhances them. You may not believe the old adage at Christmas time, but when dealing with your followers, it is better for you, as a leader, to give than to receive.

17. *Keep your goal in sight.* Remember, the goal is to convert your dream to reality; leadership is merely one tool in your entrepreneurial kit. Unfortunately, leadership is a potential opiate. Some people get so caught up in the power of leadership, aiming all their energy at the next hit, that their true efforts are distracted and their goal gets distorted. Watch out! It's easy to get hooked.

18. *One-to-one is the same as 1-million-to-1-million.* Don't prejudge whether your followers are risk averse. Some people won't take on a 1-million-to-1-million risk-reward ratio because they won't be able to pay up if they lose. That doesn't necessarily make them risk averse. They might take the same odds if the dollar amount were lower.

In addition, if you can change the amounts (from 1 million to 100,000, for example), you may seem all the more a leader to those who rejected those odds at higher amounts. That's one way to establish your leadership stature.

19. *Trust.* I'm not referring to integrity. That requirement goes without saying, and your due diligence must pinpoint honesty that deserves moral trust. By trust, I refer to a level of confidence that lets you allow your followers to do what's needed. Other types of leaders seem able to do this rather easily; it's more difficult for entrepreneurs. After all, you're not asking for volunteers to follow a standard operating procedure manual or the *Bible* or a play book. You're seeking people who can follow something more amorphous than clouds, harder to grasp than mercury, and about as clear as a picture projected toward the midnight sky. No one can see your dream, except through you, and when you change it, followers may not recognize it. Yet, you must trust them to do their part well. To do that, you must do your part well, by keeping the picture of your dream clear, visible, and comprehensible. Then, let them do their thing, but watch how they do it.

Bob Galvin described his father as someone who treated people with intense discipline and with trust. "He had an ability to convey the right blend of giving an order and demonstrating that he trusted you, which was an immensely motivating factor," Bob said. To do so requires that you have a very clear picture of your dream and how you plan to make it real.

20. *Communicate to inspire.* Your communication must inspire your followers. Your communication will inspire if you remember how much you want your dream and if you realize how much you need your followers to make your dream real. Then, demonstrate that. Your sacrifices for the goal, your willingness to risk and to bear responsibility and possibly public humiliation can be far more inspiring than how you speak. Just don't keep your feelings secret and don't think for a moment that you can do it all alone—or you may have to.

21. *Be a cheerleader.* Many authors have said that entrepreneurs must be cheerleaders, cheering on their dreams. That's true, but there is more to it. Watch cheerleaders in a stadium or arena. They give their all, aiming their efforts at tens of thousands of people, even though a very small part of the audience seems aroused or inspired by their cheers. The response of those few is sufficient, and a few responses must also suffice for you. Your cheerleading will be aimed at many people, and even though only a few will respond, you can't become discouraged by the underwhelming reaction. After all, it isn't Amateur Hour, where the prize goes to the one receiving the most applause. Your goal is to land those followers that will make your dreams real. So, pinpoint your cheerleading at each prospective follower and steel yourself for the deaf ear most will turn.

22. *Remember what they wish they were.* I agree with Jim Covert that, deep down, "everybody would love to be an entrepreneur." It's much like the autumnal emergence of armchair quarterbacks. All of us would like to be quarterbacks, but some, lacking the talent or guts to do that, follow (electronically but nonetheless devotedly) their favorite quarterback and, as fans, believe they participate in moving the ball forward.

For your followers, being in the shadow of your entrepreneurial pursuits may be the closest they can come to being entrepreneurs. You are giving them the chance to do indirectly what they can't do alone. This is the closest they can come. You will be making their day, and they will strive to repay that favor, if you remember why they are there.

23. *Do windows but not details.* Earlier I told you about Elmer Stokes*, my client who was his own janitorial service, and

Margie Korshak, who seals envelopes or "whatever it takes." That pattern was consistent throughout my dealings with and interviews with entrepreneurs. Unlike many managers who strive to distinguish themselves through their duties, entrepreneurial leaders distinguish themselves through their dreams and will do anything to make them real. If your dream is all-important, getting your hands dirty is immaterial; it might even feel good. Some have dual talents and can lead the details of day-to-day operation while expanding the reality of their dreams; most are best at the entrepreneurial stage. Know your strengths and weaknesses and act accordingly.

Nothing increases a follower's dedication more than seeing how much his or her leader cares. Perhaps the prime example of an entrepreneur who mastered that is the late Sam Walton, the founder of Wal-Mart. While in his seventies and undergoing chemotherapy for bone cancer, Walton rose before dawn to read spreadsheets, flew from city to city to visit stores and talk with the hourly paid employees. He told them, by his down-home words, his showman style, and his personal sacrifice, dedication, commitment, and concern, that the business was still important to him. They knew that he was worth over $20 billion and that he didn't have to care. But they also knew he did care and that he was asking them to care. They responded with results.

Point of Information

Ethics and Attitudes

When real estate and publishing entrepreneur Mort Zuckerman took over the ailing *Daily News* in January 1993, many senior reporters and columnists got what they called their "death warrants"—thin envelopes stuffed with pink slips. In all, 170 of the paper's Newspaper Guild members learned their fate in this manner.

Those who were kept got thicker envelopes, but staying was a mixed blessing. They were to receive far less money than before, in some cases $450 a week less. Many of the oldest and best paid employees were dropped. Reason: The savings are greater by far per capita when you keep younger employees, who are far less well paid.

The issue, says Mort Zuckerman, was survival. The *Daily News* once had the largest daily circulation of any newspaper in the United States. Then hard times reduced the *News* to an echo of the feisty paper that had been the breakfast tradition for a million New Yorkers. Was he wrong to fire these people, some with 35 years of loyal service to the newspaper? From a human point of view, undoubtedly. But from an entrepreneur's point of view, decidedly not. Zuckerman saved the paper. Without his $36 million infusion of capital and the guts to make the tough decisions, the *Daily News* would have been history.

Looked at in the most positive light, Zuckerman secured the jobs of the remaining 1500 *Daily News* workers in a city without substitute jobs. It takes a determined man to rescue a company from certain death. And Zuckerman stepped up to the plate.

Chances are you will never have to take similar steps. But when the boat is sinking, the teak chest goes over the side. Just pray you can operate without layoffs.

There are some who advise entrepreneurs to operate their businesses by doing unto others as they would have others do unto them. A humanistic approach is a style that pays dividends for some entrepreneurs. Jerry Reinsdorf, founder of Balcor and owner of the Chicago Bulls and Chicago White Sox, told me about signing one of his team's draft choices, when the player's options were limited. "I know we could have made a better deal. I had the guy boxed. But it would be the wrong thing to do because, sometime down the road, he'll have a choice to get even with me. So it wasn't that I was being good. I was being selfish." Every entrepreneur needs all the help he or she can get during the inevitable hard times.

Do all entrepreneurs live by the golden rule? Of course not. Different strokes for different folks. Jerry Reinsdorf believes that "the golden rule is a pretty good rule. At the same time, you have to be alert to the fact that most people don't have the same beliefs that you do. You have to be alert [so] that people don't take advantage of you." Some entrepreneurs are not just unkind, they are ruthless. They don't pay their bills, and they even stiff the weaker suppliers they work with. Years ago, when still a fledgling, Financial News Network was such a slow pay that the electric company once sent workers to shut off the power in mid-broadcast. (An FNN apprentice raced to the bank for the cash Con Ed demanded.)

When tough businesspeople bother justifying their actions, they mention the survival of the fittest. They do provide jobs, after all. The founder of an enormous U.S. business that is the envy of almost everyone once agreed to buy a small business from a much older man for $3 million. The price was agreed to after a tough, arms-length negotiation. The buyer also agreed to write the manual that the buyers of the product would need to understand the product. Later, the older man called to say the final payment was $250,000 short. The young genius quipped, "You didn't think I was going to write the manual for nothing, now, did you?"

I'll leave it to you to decide which style works for you. There are probably as many ruthless entrepreneurs out there as those who follow the golden rule.

Entrepreneurial leadership, like other forms of leadership, entails a blend of what is ethically correct and what is financially successful. One must be prepared for the stimulation and the responsibility of the position. This chapter has detailed numerous steps you can take. I also suggest that you carefully consider what brand of leadership you would need to see in an entrepreneur you would follow (hypothetically, of course, since your goal is to be the entrepreneur who does the leading).

16

You Have
What It Takes

A man he seems of confident tomorrows.
WILLIAM WORDSWORTH

You can become an entrepreneur no matter what your IQ, genetic pattern, physical abilities or disabilities, sibling birth order, or gender. Don't get me wrong, entrepreneurs are special people, but before they become entrepreneurs, they are ordinary people. They don't have something special in their genes; anyone can learn to be an entrepreneur. You don't have to be born a certain way or have a particular capacity. You can learn everything you need to be an entrepreneur. Clearly, entrepreneurs are made not born. All you need is a desire and willingness to learn. You must be alert, directed, and purposeful. Those attributes will be easier to attain if you remember these lessons:

1. *Becoming an entrepreneur is no accident.* If you see your dream, go for it purposefully. Prepare for entrepreneurship, and, when your dream surfaces, if the best way for you to deal with your dream is entrepreneurship, then, by all means, choose that vehicle.

2. *Opportunities surround you.* Think about your surroundings— your hobbies, habits, your employer's business and its daily

processes and tools, your home and its daily processes and tools, your family and their needs, you and your fantasies and desires, and anything else that interests you. They all contain opportunities. You are present in all those arenas, not by accident but because something drew you to those people, places, and events. Whatever drew you there, whatever makes you learn to know and love them, is also what makes them suitable places to find your entrepreneurial opportunity.

3. *Find the switch that lights the way.* Seeing and seizing opportunities is no accident. To paraphrase Thomas Edison, success is 1 percent inspiration and 99 percent perspiration. Professor Mort Kamien, of Northwestern University's Kellogg School, would add a possible additional ingredient, desperation, the kind that comes from losing your job. That desperation is a good example of a switch that turns on our senses and mind to spot and grab opportunities that often were there all along. It sometimes takes something extra to make an entrepreneur see what was always there. That's no accident.

"Well, you're on your own now." Those words raise different reactions in different people. Some fear being responsible or having their performance exposed. Others are exhilarated by the challenge and the ability to determine their own destiny and make their dream real in a very public arena. You may have more than one of those feelings; many people—even many entrepreneurs—do.

That combination of emotions—of fear and exhilaration—is common, whether you're starting a new business or going away to college. At first, you may find it confusing, but that combination is good. It gives you two sources of adrenaline: (1) the exhilaration that comes from realizing your potential, and (2) the motivation that you generate to deal with fear of failure. These are the traits that will help you get the job done.

Apply Your Common Sense

History is replete with examples of people who had little or no formal education but who were immensely successful as entrepreneurs. I have been reluctant to dwell on such examples because I never want to influence anyone to forgo any education. First of all, you may not become an entrepreneur or you may not make it as one, in which case a good education may be critical. Second, as technology and business complexity increase, the chances decrease for undereducated entrepreneurs to succeed.

Much has been written hypothesizing whether certain undereducated entrepreneurs would have done as well if they had been "burdened" with more formal education. I'm not sure of the answer. It would be easy to argue that some kinds of education prohibit free flowing thoughts, thus blocking the ability to have different dreams. I don't agree. The exceptions clearly disprove such a rule, even if they don't quite prove a contrary one.

I admit that some businesses don't require their entrepreneurs to have much education. However, as our society and the global business community expand their size and sophistication, entrepreneurs need better skills to remain competitive. So, if it's available and possible, continue your formal education. If your opportunity ripens before you finish school, measure whether the opportunity can be preserved until your skills have reached the necessary levels. If you're sure the opportunity will rot, then measure what you might lose against what the education might add to your life.

Education is important, but no amount of formal education is as important to entrepreneurs as common sense. Life is filled with those unexpected circumstances. Although formal education can help you deal with some problems, many— especially the new and different ones—require the ability to react quickly, positively, simply, and effectively. To do that requires common sense. How do you get it? Pay attention to what you are doing, how effective you are, and how other people relate to both. Also, notice what other successful people do, how what they're doing works, and how others react to their achievements. It even pays to do the same with less successful people, so that common sense can also tell you what not to do.

Enjoy!

Entrepreneuring isn't easy, but I've never met an entrepreneur who didn't enjoy it. So, be ready for a tough grind. But enjoy the trip. You should; after all, it's to your dream.

I have entered on an enterprise which is without precedent.—Jean Jacques Rousseau

17

Chase the Dream—
Not the Rainbow

We chase rainbows as children figuring there is a pot of gold at the other end. The rainbow always fades before we get there. Even when we grow up, preoccupation with the real pot of gold, or money, is understandable. In fact, it is universal. As Jerry Goodman, or "Adam Smith," explains in his classic book, *The Money Game,* money is the way we keep score.

But don't be led astray. Let your accountant keep score, unless you prefer to be an accountant and not an entrepreneur. Focus on keeping score and you won't find success. As an entrepreneur, success is your goal. Focus on your dream and you may well succeed. If so, the money will come.

Debbi Fields told me she gets letters from children who want to make a million dollars. She advises them to "do something because you love it; don't just pursue dollars." She says "I never do it for the money," and she quotes her husband, Randy: "If you chase money, you won't catch it. What people ought to strive to be is successful. Do what you do really well, then money will find you."

Joe Sullivan, the former president of Swift and founder of his own business, said, "Making a million dollars never was a be all and end all. It just never has been a very important thing. The money was more a sign of being able to be successful. Money itself is not important to me." Joe's position and successes project images of tycoons riding in chauffeured limousines.

Actually, Joe drives a seven-year-old Volvo that, he says, runs very well. For Joe, his financial numbers are sufficient score keeping. Others may require the trappings that shout out the score.

Jack Reynolds, the former NBC news reporter who recently founded his own production company, told me that, "as an employee for the network, I kept score by my work product—each project I completed was a notch on my score card. As an entrepreneur, money becomes the score-keeping mechanism."

Many people believe that a big difference between entrepreneurs and corporate managers is that entrepreneurs work harder because they have more to gain (implying that they do it to gain more money). That's false on several counts. Many managers work harder and make more than many entrepreneurs. And although most entrepreneurs do work hard, they don't do it just to make more money. They have a higher purpose. Entrepreneurs really do have their own work ethic.

If entrepreneurs did it for the money—for what the money could buy for them—it would be difficult to explain the continuing entrepreneurial exploits of people like the late Sam Walton, Sam LeFrak, Jay Pritzker, Ross Perot, Michael Smurfit, or Lester Crown. Each of them has accumulated extraordinary wealth and there is little they could not afford to buy. Jay Pritzker told me he continued his entrepreneurial pursuits because he's a "crazy deal junkie." Jay noted that he didn't need the money. The money had nothing to do with it, except in the scoring.

Sam LeFrak is a preeminent builder who developed Lefrak City, a New York apartment complex housing thousands of people. Sam now owns over 100,000 apartments, an acre on 57th Street between 5th and 6th Avenues in Manhattan, and many other valuable properties and businesses. All his building activities are grounded in the tradition of his grandfather, a builder, and his father, an architect, who started developing homes in the 1920s. Sam was introduced to the family business at age 8 and became its president in the late 1940s.

Sam LeFrak told me that "Life isn't a big yawn. Life is a series of challenges. I haven't yawned in 20 years; the word 'tired' is not in my vocabulary." Sam's mother used to ask him, "Why are you working so hard?" Sam would say, "You know what is hap-

pening today won't be here tomorrow and I'm getting fulfillment." Sam told me that he worked hard because he wanted to,
certainly not because of any economic reasons. He does things
because he can do things and achieve things. That is Sam's motivation.

Michael Smurfit, chair of the Jefferson Smurfit Group in
Ireland, doesn't need more money. Yet, when his company's
dealings with Venezuela required attention, he flew to Caracas,
despite the unrest there, to meet with the president. He depart-
ed just two hours before an attempted coup. He told me that he
would do it again because he loves what he does. The business
is, after all, his baby; he has changed its nerve structure totally
since he inherited it. His commitment has nothing to do with
money.

No, those entrepreneurs don't do it just for the money. But
what about the small fry, just-getting-started entrepreneurs?
What about those, such as the laid off or the immigrants, who
can't get a good job and see entrepreneurship as an available
alternative to make ends meet?

Of course, there are people who start with a dream of riches
and then try to find the vehicle to make a bundle. Most of them
are blinded by the money, which causes them to select the
wrong dream, to stretch for opportunities where wise people
would not tread, to neglect basics, to falter and fail. Of the hundreds of entrepreneurs I've interviewed and represented, very
few have been in it primarily for the money, and most of those
who were have failed.

Some entrepreneurs talk about money as a goal, but penetrat-
ing questions can prove revealing. For example, Sam Zell said
"making money has always been a motivating force for me."
However, that was said while Sam was discussing his childhood. He went on to say that he "recognized quite early that
there's a correlation between money and power and having
resources gave me the ability [as a child] to better control my
life, to generate freedom which was very important." So, like
Debbi Fields and so many other entrepreneurs, money was
Sam's ticket to independently controlling his life. Money was
their vehicle, not their destination.

18
When to
Stop Dreaming

Starting a business has been compared to having a baby. Actually, marriage is a better metaphor. Under that scenario, your dream is a date. Mature dating means learning all you can about your date's qualities, your compatibility, what you can do for each other, and whether "this is it." However, until you take the final step, there is no commitment. The same is true of your dream. Be devoted, but not blindly. Be positive and do all you can to make your dream a reality, but at the same time, watch for signs that it won't work.

Staying objective about your dream isn't easy but it's necessary. Here are some red flags that could justify abandoning your dream:

1. *The market doesn't love it as much as you do.* But be sure there isn't another market for the same product or service and check your market research or marketing approach. Changing your approach or having someone else market your product may be a solution.

2. *The window of opportunity is shut.* Although some businesses are eclipsed by interim events, such as new inventions, others go in cycles. So be sure to ascertain whether the window is permanently or temporarily closed.

3. *The dream is great, but you're the wrong person to implement it.* Obvious solutions include obtaining a new partner, selling

the idea for cash or royalties, or joint venturing with a company with suitable financial strength and management capabilities in production, marketing, sales, and distribution.

4. *By pursuing more than one dream, you are pulled in too many directions, dangerously diluting your efforts.* Times change, often rather quickly. So too must your dream. Be certain, though, that you are merely altering your existing dream and not diluting it with another one.

Even after you have implemented your dream—entered into the marriage—there are appropriate times to consider divorce:

1. The cycle is over.
2. Your interest has waned.
3. You are a good entrepreneur but a lousy manager.
4. It's time already.

Sam Zell once told me, "When everyone is buying, I want to be selling, and when everyone is selling, I want to be buying." That's great advice, but running contrary to cycles means you must be able to spot the trends and buck the crowd. The key to following Sam's advice is having great self-confidence. Otherwise, even if you see the trend, you won't be confident enough to believe in what you see.

Jerry Reinsdorf, the founder of Balcor, a real estate syndicator and developer, built his company into a great success story. While everyone was preparing for even greater growth in the real estate industry, Reinsdorf sold Balcor to Shearson American Express for well over a hundred million dollars. Many of his competitors who were building for continuing good times are also in retirement but not by their own choice. They were toppled by the 1986 Tax Act, the savings and loan debacle, and the resulting recession. Of course, Reinsdorf did not really retire. He now heads the Chicago Bulls and the Chicago White Sox, activities that became his new passion, causing his interest in Balcor to wane and influencing his decision to sell. Talk about timing, he sold his real estate company before the crash and bought the Bulls in their lackluster pre–Michael Jordan days.

Entrepreneurship is a unique—but very obtainable—talent. So is managing. Some people are blessed with both. Bankruptcy court records are replete with examples of those who aren't. Most of them could have salvaged something if they were able to admit that they needed help. They might have had to divorce themselves from their business by resigning or even selling out (often more difficult than stopping their dream), but at least they would have had some "alimony" to show for their efforts.

Sam Metzger was a successful lawyer who became involved on a part-time basis in several businesses, including toy manufacturing, art galleries, and publishing, all of which did quite well. In 1980, Metzger gave up his profitable law practice to cofound Chipwich, a company that made ice cream sandwiches and sold them from carts near New York's Fifth Avenue.

When Metzger was involved to a limited extent as an entrepreneur, spotting and grabbing opportunities but having other people run them, he prospered. Even Chipwich's beginning was immensely successful, and Chipwich quickly became a household word. However, when Metzger gave up everything else and focused completely on Chipwich, he watched his business go into bankruptcy. Was something wrong with Metzger's focus? Was he a successful generalist and unsuccessful specialist? As a full-time practicing lawyer, he didn't have the time to get involved in management. When he left law for full-time involvement at Chipwich, his focus shifted from goals to the day-to-day techniques of managing. He stopped focusing solely on seizing or converting that dream to reality. He changed his focus from where he was going to how he was getting there—in other words, to management, which required different talents. That change in focus resulted in his change of fortune.

Most entrepreneurs feel they can't afford the luxury of leaving their business. In reality, many entrepreneurs are not good managers and, therefore, can't afford not to leave their businesses. Even if you are an entrepreneur with managerial skills, you may have to step away, periodically, from managing to give yourself space to dream again.

There is no alarm clock that tells you, "It's time already." You have to be wise enough to know the right time to call it quits. Sometimes, you get in trouble trying to tell someone else, "It's time already." That's what happened when Robert Haft told his father, the majority stockholder of their family business (Dart Stores, Crown Books, etc.), that he was retired. As a result, the Haft family now spends much of their time with lawyers and judges.

I have been called on by clients to break the news that "It's time already." Quite frequently, it takes a measure of subtlety and diplomacy. You may recall my story about Pop, the elderly owner of the large marina that my clients bought. Shortly after I negotiated for my clients to buy Pop's marina, one of my clients alerted me that Pop had contacted him to say the deal was off. Pop was facing the trauma that most entrepreneurs eventually face—letting his baby go. I immediately went to see him.

We met at his house, which adjoined the marina. At this point, Pop found it more difficult to get about and used a golf cart to get around his property. We got in the cart and drove through the marina. It was a project as long as a city block. I got him talking about the marina as usual. But when we were halfway across the marina I said "Pop, I can't let my people do this deal. The more you talk about it, the more I see what a 'hands on' business this is. My clients are in Chicago. They can't run it from there." He was shocked. He meant to sell and was only wavering. I paused to let it sink in and then said, "It'd be different if someone could watch over it for us. Any chance we could hire you?" "Well, yeah!" he said. "Then," I said, "we'll have to redo the contract—so you can keep the golf cart." We wrapped up the deal quickly. Pop smiled broadly. He had won visiting right to his child, which made "It's time already" more acceptable.

Listen to the Sounds and Silences

How can you learn when to stop dreaming? There is no scientific formula for knowing when. If you listen to sounds and silences, you will know when. Let me explain.

When associates in my law firm ask me when they will be ready to become a partner in the firm, I tell them, "You and I will both know because we will be told by others." Sometimes, clients call and compliment the associate's work. Occasionally, third parties—accountants, cocounsel, opposing counsel, bankers, or investment bankers—will tell me how well things have gone. More often, I hear by silence, when these people are secure enough with the associates to call them and not me.

The same is true for you. Listen hard and you will know when to abandon your dream or when to start converting your dream to reality.

Why Entrepreneurs Try, Try Again

Jay Pritzker is a principal in the Hyatt Hotels chain and a self-described deal junkie. Jay owns or has a hand in dozens of businesses.

Phil Romano founded Romano's Macaroni Grill. But first he sold Fuddruckers, his famous upscale hamburger chain.

Howard Ruff lost everything in an Evelyn Wood Reading Dynamics regional franchise but then went on to success with his lucrative newsletter, *Ruff Times.*

There it is: three entrepreneurs and three common incentives for trying again: Pritzker's collector instinct, Romano's restlessness, and Ruff's persistence.

Collectors gather up many businesses. Some of them develop synergistic units that support their main businesses, the way Hugh Hefner did in elaborating on the Playboy theme with logo-embossed merchandise, book publishing, key clubs, and, more recently, video units. Others will buy into anything that appeals to them like ITT's former chair, Harold Geneen, or Sam Zell.

Then there are the restless who will sell the bird in hand to pursue the two in the bush, even if the odds are less favorable this time around. And there are the persistent, who are as appealing as any of the others because they never give up.

In virtually all these cases, the underlying motivation is the compulsion to succeed. Pride forces each entrepreneur to keep on keeping on. They are all drawn by the siren song of what New York sophisticates used to refer to, laconically, as that "bitch goddess Success." Each of the repeaters also expressed image concerns.

When Phil Romano sold Fuddruckers, he didn't enjoy sitting in his big house on the hill. He had to start another business. His wife had reservations. She said, "Why do you have to do it? If it fails, everybody will think you were lucky the first time." Phil didn't think about failure. He was out to prove his success wasn't a fluke.

Ruff went bankrupt and worried that the loss would influence how he and his family were perceived. He was out to prove his failure was a fluke. Two different cases: One a roaring success, the other ended in bankruptcy. Both were determined to try again. Who were these fellows trying to impress? Who do entrepreneurs generally mean to impress? Themselves? Their parents—whether dead or alive? Their spouses? The boss they fire? (Not Phil Romano. He was so unemployable, he chose to go into business right after college.)

Actually, the motivations of entrepreneurs are complex. Most of them share several of these motivations. It doesn't really matter whose perceptions they are out to change. What does matter is that entrepreneurs are concerned about their image.

The collectors, like Jay Pritzker, LeFrak, and Zell, aren't too different. They never rest on their laurels. No matter how many successes they have, they still have more to prove. Their motivations are also complex. Some fear they will be perceived as having succeeded in good times. They have to prove they can also do it in hard times.

If the perception is that they succeeded because of the help of others, they must show they were pivotal to their own success. If the perception is that they started with an existing business, they have to show they can start from scratch.

Perhaps the perception is that they succeeded because they chose an industry whose time was ripe. They must correct that perception by succeeding in a different business when the time is not ripe—or show how smart they are by selecting another one when it is ripe. All these motivations reflect deeply felt needs for entrepreneurs.

If you share these motivations, you too will need to try, try again—even if you fail the first or second time out. As the wealthy Chicago industrialist, Lester Crown, puts it, only half in jest, "Six people failed before there was 7-Up."

Sue Ling Gin accepts persistence, saying, "You've got to fail four times to get to the fifth time when you will be successful." Either way, you must be confident even if the odds are so long that others scoff at you. That is a hallmark of an entrepreneur.

About the Author

Lloyd E. Shefsky is the founder and a member of Shefsky &
Froelich Ltd., a Chicago-based law firm. He specializes in
representing entrepreneurs and is nationally recognized as
an expert on entrepreneurship. Mr. Shefsky is a director of
the Illinois Institute for Entrepreneurship Education.

Index